ISBN 978-1-331-80677-6
PIBN 10237272

This book is a reproduction of an important historical work. Forgotten Books uses
state-of-the-art technology to digitally reconstruct the work, preserving the original format
whilst repairing imperfections present in the aged copy. In rare cases, an imperfection in
the original, such as a blemish or missing page, may be replicated in our edition. We do,
however, repair the vast majority of imperfections successfully; any imperfections that
remain are intentionally left to preserve the state of such historical works.

English
Français
Deutsche
Italiano
Español
Português

www.forgottenbooks.com

Mythology Photography **Fiction**
Fishing Christianity **Art** Cooking
Essays Buddhism Freemasonry
Medicine **Biology** Music **Ancient
Egypt** Evolution Carpentry Physics
Dance Geology **Mathematics** Fitness
Shakespeare **Folklore** Yoga Marketing
Confidence Immortality Biographies
Poetry **Psychology** Witchcraft
Electronics Chemistry History **Law**
Accounting **Philosophy** Anthropology
Alchemy Drama Quantum Mechanics
Atheism Sexual Health **Ancient History**
Entrepreneurship Languages Sport
Paleontology Needlework Islam
Metaphysics Investment Archaeology
Parenting Statistics Criminology
Motivational

WELL OF WATER
SPRINGING UP INTO
EVERLASTING LIFE

GOD'S MONUMENT
TO
THE CHRISTIAN

GOD'S MONUMENT TO THE CHRISTIAN.

See page 56.

THROUGH THE EYE TO THE HEART;

OR,

EYE-TEACHING IN THE SUNDAY-SCHOOL.

By Rev. W. F. CRAFTS.

["CALLENE FISK."]

WITH AN INTRODUCTION BY J. H. VINCENT, D.D.,

AND

AN APPENDIX FOR INFANT-CLASS TEACHERS

By MISS SARA J. TIMANUS.

"Open thou mine eyes, that I may behold wondrous things out of thy law."

———◆———

NEW YORK:

NELSON & PHILLIPS.

CINCINNATI: HITCHCOCK & WALDEN.

TO MY FATHER,

REV. F. A. CRAFTS,

WHO LED ME TO CHRIST BOTH BY WHAT I *HEARD* FROM

HIS LIPS, AND WHAT I *SAW* IN HIS LIFE,

This Book is lovingly Dedicated.

INTRODUCTION.

THIS volume on the power and method of "Eye-teaching," which I am requested to "introduce to the Sunday-school public," needs no words of explanation or compliment. Its pages speak for themselves. The book is a defense of a most ancient method of teaching—so old that we cannot recall the time when men who thought and taught at all did not employ it. We find it in Eden, when God gave man his first command ; at Sinai, when Moses taught God's chosen people both law and gospel by complicated and impressive symbols; in Israel, by the Hiddekel, and in Babylon, when holy prophets gave forth burning words from the invisible God; in Galilee and in Judea, when He who "spake as never man spake" taught the thronging multitudes the love and power and sweetness that were to be found in his own divine Gospel. Prophets, priests, apostles, philosophers, reformers, and teachers of all ages and of every nation, have used it. To-day, in the primary school, the academy, college, on the popular rostrum, and in every court of justice, it is continually employed.

This book is more than a defense. It is a guide-book to all the practical details of the art. If the author errs at all it is in the excess of examples which he furnishes. He illustrates the whole field of illustration. One is left in no doubt as to what he means by a principle or a definition. He also exposes many of the mistakes which enthusiasts in chalk have made, reminding the teacher that things thoroughly good may be sadly abused.

The contribution of Miss Sara J. Timanus is not the least valuable part of this valuable hand-book.

Let not those who use "Through the Eye to the Heart" forget that after all it is the SPIRIT, and not alone the truth, that is to reach and regenerate and enrich the heart. The clear apprehension of truth does not necessarily bring the affections and the life into harmony with the truth. For this interior and divine and most essential work we stand in daily need, both as teachers and pupils, of the "Holy Ghost sent down from heaven." For this gift—for this TEACHER who shall "teach us all things"—let us look with the faith that is the " evidence of things not seen." J. H. VINCENT.

NEW YORK, *March*, 1873.

PREFACE.

An effort has been made to glean from standard Sabbath-school periodicals and the labors of prominent workers in convention, as well as from special contributors and my own experience, such hints upon Eye-Teaching and examples of its use as may be valuable to Sunday-school teachers.

The exercises will be found to be brief and suggestive rather than elaborate and exhaustive, the desire being to stimulate thought and study rather than take their place.

I wish to make due acknowledgment to "Object and Outline Teaching" by Rev. Henry M'Cook, D.D.; also to the current numbers of THE BLACKBOARD, edited by Samuel W. Clark, for some excellent lessons culled from them.

I desire that all my friends who have so kindly contributed lessons may feel that my gratitude rests upon them.

W. F. C.

HAVERHILL, MASS.

CONTENTS.

THROUGH THE EYE TO THE HEART.

EYE-TEACHING IN THE SUNDAY-SCHOOL.

THE great object of the Sunday-school is not to organize its members into a picnic club, or a library association, or a singing-school, or a theological institute ; not merely to please, or discipline, or teach, as the *end* in view, but by *means* of all these to accomplish its great purpose, TO PRESENT CHRIST TO THE HEARTS OF THE SCHOOL.

Christ is to be the Alpha and Omega, the beginning and the ending, the first and the last, in Sunday-school work. He must be above all, and in all, and through all the exercises.

A little child climbed up in her chair at home to preach to her little brothers and sisters. She turned to the right and said, " Jesus ; " then to the front and said, " Jesus ; " then to the left and said, " Jesus," and her sermon was ended. So in the Sunday-school we must begin and continue and end with " Jesus."

Though a school can speak at concerts with the tongues of men and of angels, and though its blackboard be always attractive, its superintendent always pleasant, and its numbers large, yet if it only talks *about* Christ instead of *talking Christ*, if it only *pleases* without *saving* its scholars, all its machinery and outward success are but as " sounding brass and a tinkling cymbal." Like one of the English light-houses, the Sunday-school should have the double inscription, " *To give light, to save life.*" A boy with a Testament was asked what he knew about Jesus. He replied, "I haven't got to that yet." A Sunday-school which has not "got to that yet," amid its many schemes and plans and picnics, is false to its trust.

To PRESENT CHRIST, then, is our object in Sunday-school work. How shall we vividly and savingly present him to the heart? By universal consent the senses must usher truth to the soul.

The Sunday-school works mainly through the two most influential senses, sight and hearing. Hearing lacks vividness without sight; sight lacks definiteness without hearing. It is well, therefore, that hearing and seeing should accompany each other. Joseph's brethren brought to their father, who had long mourned for Joseph as dead, this wonderful message: "Thus saith thy son Joseph, I am yet alive; come down unto me, tarry not." Jacob's heart fainted when he simply *heard* these words, for he believed them not; but "when he *saw the wagons* which Joseph had sent to carry him, the spirit of Jacob their father revived." The wagons would have meant nothing unless they had been preceded by the message; the message would have failed unless it had been followed by the wagons. This shows us how to use the eye and ear in the Sunday-school. Give what "is *written*," and then, by maps, pictures, objects, blackboard exercises, and stories, put it into "wagons" to help the imagination and the understanding. The flowers and butterflies in "Joseph's garden" had no smile of hope, no promise of a resurrection, for Mary, when she came there at that early hour of Easter morning, "while it was *yet dark*" in her heart; but since the message has come, "The Lord is risen indeed," every flower and butterfly has been to the bereaved an object-lesson of the resurrection. Until the announcement of Christ's rising was heard, the grain gave no promise of a future life; but, after that, Paul put the whole doctrine of the resurrection into the "seed that falls into the ground and dies" that it may live again.

Thus hearing and seeing should work together. But while "Ear-Gate" has had a well-trodden path by constant use, "Eye-Gate" has rusted on its hinges in neglect. We wish to speak especially of the way to present Christ to the heart through this much-neglected "Eye-Gate."

The *visions* by which God taught his truth were usually more impressive than his *spoken messages*. The words written in fire on the wall at Babylon conveyed God's warning to the King's heart more convincingly than spoken words would have done. Dr. Vincent found it hard to get his little boy to eat bread and butter until, one morning, after spreading a slice of bread, he cut it into bread-logs and piled it up in the shape of a house, and then very quickly "down came the house," and all was eaten!

Put the "bread of heaven" into object-lessons and visible illustrations, and the little hearts who find it hard to realize the truth they hear will eagerly receive it and understand it. Talk about the power of God's promises in general terms, and it may all be forgotten. Make the picture of a key on the blackboard and write on it "Promise," and then tell the story of the "key of promise" and Doubting Castle, and you will make the oldest and youngest hearers feel the preciousness and power of God's promises; or, picture a bunch of keys of different sizes and write a promise on each one, and then you can tell those to whom you speak that God's promises fit every experience of life and unlock every difficulty—and every hearer will grasp and keep the thought.

EYE-TEACHING IS PHILOSOPHICAL.

All of the senses *seem* to merge themselves in sight. As each of the four fingers is exactly opposite the thumb, so each of the other four senses seems to connect itself with sight. We say of food that we have been describing, "*Taste and see;*" we say of the fragrance of a flower of which we have been speaking, "*Smell and see;*" we say of some excellent singer whose voice we have eulogized, "*Hear and see;*" or of a gem we have called very smooth, "*Feel and see.*" In a new sense, "It is *all in your eye.*" Whether it be music or perfume, we say, "*Come and see;*" whether it be bread or stone, we say, "Try and *see.*" Even of questions in our minds we say, "Let me *see;*" and if the matter be obscure, "I can't *see* it." This is because *we think by images*, by something we can *see*, or *imagine that we see.* It is a craving of the mind that makes "the *likes*" necessary in every kind of teaching. The unknown must be taught by *likening* it to something that is known; the unseen must be represented by the seen.

Modern primers teach the unknown word by placing it beside the picture of the object it represents. The picture of a dog will aid the little scholar to remember the word "Dog." We used to say, "D stands for Dog;" rather was it "Dog (the picture) stands for D." Half of our childhood knowledge comes in rhymes about the "*likes.*" Rev. Dr. M'Cook gives a happy example of this in his work on "Object and Outline Teaching:"

> "As red as a cherry, as brisk as a bee,
> As brown as a berry, as tall as a tree,
> As sweet as a pink, as bitter as gall,
> As black as ink, as round as a ball," etc.

Try to teach a child what "red" is without this implied or real object-teaching, with nothing but words to describe what it is, and the child will have as poor an idea of it as the blind man, who, after a long explanation of this color, concluded it must be "*very much like the sound of a trumpet.*" Hold up the cherry to the child, and the lesson is learned in a moment. This same method follows us into a completer education. Maps, specimens, blackboards, slates, etc., are found even in the highest grades of teaching. Though a man have spoken his words never so eloquently, the hearers want him, if possible, to have "*something to show for it.*" A figure is more easily retained than an abstract truth. So deeply grounded is this fact in our nature that we think by figures and pictures. Indeed, language itself is *fossil pictures*, rather than "fossil poetry," as Emerson calls it. Letters were originally hieroglyphics, and hieroglyphics are only pictures used as symbols. When we add something *shown* to something *spoken*, we only add a picture for the eye to a picture for the imagination.

EYE-TEACHING SCRIPTURAL.

Dr. Vincent, in the preface to his recent work on "The Church School," says : "The good philanthropists of the last century, in digging that they might build a human fabric, laid bare an ancient and divine foundation." These words, spoken of the modern Sunday-school, are especially true of its eye-teaching. It is not "a new idea," but an "ancient and divine foundation" laid bare for us to build upon to-day.

The Bible is full of object-lessons taught by God himself, by Christ, and by the inspired writers, with trees, stars, shields, girdles, fruits, birds, pictures, etc., as their texts and illustrations. The broken tree teaches the fate of the wicked, the withered tree that of the idle, the fruitful tree that of the righteous. The "empty vine" teaches us of the unfaithful, the vine of "wild grapes" of the wicked, the vine of "good fruit" of those who abide in Christ. The star represents the Messiah, also those who turn many to righteousness. The rent garment, the rotten girdle, the "naughty figs," etc., are used to represent wickedness and God's dealings with it. In fact, the Bible is an "illuminated missal," as Chapin calls it, in every page full of pictures and object-teaching.

God himself is our precedent in this kind of instruction. Take, for instance, his teachings of Jeremiah, "*What seest thou*, Jeremiah?" (Jer. i, 11; xxiv, 3;) or his great object-lesson given to Peter on the housetop at Joppa, (Acts x, 9, etc.) Any one interested in following out this study may find other cases where God himself taught his truth by this method of eye-teaching in the following passages, many of which the teacher can adapt to his own use

Jer. xiii, 1–11, The marred girdle; xviii, 1–6, The potter's vessel; xix, 1–11, The broken bottle; xxvii, 1–11, Bonds and yokes; xliii, 8–10, Stones in the clay; li, 63, 64, The stone and the book; Ezek. iv, 1–8, Blackboard exercise on a tile; v, The hair and the punishment of wrong; xxxvii, 1–14, Dry bones; xxxvii, 15–28, Sticks; xlvii, 1–12, Waters; Dan. ii, 31–45, The great image; Gen. ii, 16, 17, Teaching the knowledge of good and evil by means of commands associated with a tree; Jonah iv, 4–11, God's pity for the wicked taught with a gourd; Gen. xxii, 1–14, A dramatic object-lesson to teach trust in God.

The illustrations of eye-teaching in the life of our "Great Teacher" are no less abundant. Wayside wells, mountain lilies, flying clouds, vineyards, harvest-fields, every thing that met his eye, was turned into Gospel, as Midas turned every thing he touched into gold. He even caused a tree to wither away to use it as an object-lesson for his disciples! Beecher says of this act and others of his object-lessons:

"As to his condemning the tree, it was not a judicial sentence. We are not to suppose that our Saviour summoned the tree into judgment, and argued upon it as if it were a moral being under condemnation or under penalty. No; the whole plot and plan of the ancient mode of teaching forbids that interpretation of it. It is but an acted parable. And this is an important thought, because in many instances in Christ's life the same mode of teaching was resorted to.

"For example, when he cleansed the temple, undoubtedly the whole act was a parabolic act. He drove out the cattle; he overturned the money-changers' tables; he commanded those that had doves to take them thence. And the whole was not a mere formal attempt at the reformation of the administration of the temple, but a series of acts which indicated the purification of religion—the change that was going on. And, as usual, it was a kind of parabolic action. As a parable is a picture in words, conveying not a moral lesson—not a truth narrated—but simply an artificial picture, drawn for the sake of certain moral results which were to flow from it, so certain of Christ's actions were dramatic. They were, as it were, a momentary drama, enacted for the sake of the truth that they would convey. The most impressive one of all these is the Transfiguration, in which, with Peter, James, and John, he went to the mountain, where, while he was praying, they fell asleep. When they awoke they saw two angelic, or celestial personages, standing and talking with him. And his countenance was changed. Then they communed with him concerning his coming death. The whole was to those disciples a picture of the event. It was not so much a prophetic representation to interpret it to them as a pictorial representation to fortify their minds, so that when their earthly hopes, which were centered in him, should be dashed, they would be bold, and maintain faith in him. It was a kind of enacted celestial parable, or picture, or tableau.

"So here, when going in the morning to Jerusalem, Jesus saw the fig-tree and observed that it was in full leaf. Evidently it was a prematurely early one. And why should he go to see if there were figs upon it? Because sometimes a tree bore winter figs, which became ripe in early spring; and perhaps he might have expected that there would be some on that one which he might glean. But when he came to it, and found that there were no figs, but leaves only, he said, 'Let no fruit grow on thee henceforward forever, and let no man eat fruit of thee.'

"That this was said in a very impressive manner is evident by the fact that when, the day after, the disciples returned that way, they remembered the occurrence, and called his attention to the tree. Doubtless he designed that this should be a very solemn instruction to them.

"But what was the instruction? They were every day going backward and forward to and from Jerusalem. There he went into the sacred precinct, or into the part of it which was Herod's great porch—the Basilica, as it was called. There he used to

teach the people. All around about him were the insignia
of Jewish worship, and his very business was to expose the
superficialities of life in these things. He was, from day to
day, attempting to carry them back to the reality of a religious life, to a deeper moral tone, to a more earnest conscien-
tiousness. It was his business to reprehend the self-conceit
and moral complacency which passed itself off upon mere
superficial observers. And here was an opportunity. Here
happened to be, of all the trees that stood in the road on that
early spring day, one that had come into full leaf. But when
he went up to it he found no fruit on it, but leaves only—
nothing but leaves. It was just exactly like those over the
other side. All of them were full of leaves, but not one of
them—neither priest, nor scribe, nor Pharisee, nor Sadducee
—bore any fruit. All of them were clothed with leaves, but
none of them were fruitful. Here was a symbol, here was an
opportunity of illustrating a fact by a parabolic action. By
destroying that tree with a word he could impress upon his
disciples that which would be a benefit to them in their teachings of men for ever after. And he did it."

Study the sermon on the mount with a view of observing
its eye-teaching. The Emancipation Proclamation has been
so written that the shading of the letters forms a picture of
President Lincoln, which seems to lie beneath the writing. So
in this sermon on the mount, by the vividness of its local illustrations, we see a picture of Christ sitting on the mountain,
and pointing with his finger to the objects in sight, as he draws
from each its appropriate lesson; and not only do we see the
finger of Christ, but in and under the sermon we find a map
of the scenery all about him, with its cities, its trees, its birds,
its flowers, and even its weeds, sketched upon it.

Notice the sermon in this light. Wishing to impress upon
the disciples their great responsibility and wide influence, he
points them to the city of Safed on the mountains near by,
distinctly seen, as the sunlight gilded its walls, and then he
says to the disciples, " Ye are the light of the world, *a city*

that is set on a hill that cannot be hid." Matt. v, 14. Then he turns and calls the attention of the multitude to the narrow and wide gates of the city.* Through the narrow gate, which is called "the needle's eye," are passing a few foot-passengers, and a camel now and then enters, but only by bowing down and leaving his burden outside the gate : on the other hand, through the large city gates flows the gulf stream of business and the eager multitude of tradesmen. Christ applies the scene to his sermon : "Enter ye in at the strait gate : for wide is the gate, and broad is the way, that leadeth to destruction, and many there be which go in thereat : because strait is the gate, and narrow is the way, which leadeth unto life, and few there be that find it." Matt. vii, 13, etc. Beware, O ye rich men ! for you can only enter the kingdom of heaven as the camel passes the needle's eye, by bowing at the gate, and leaving your burden behind.

Then he seems to turn his eyes more to the natural objects about him, and translates their lessons to the disciples. The sparrows that sing among the olive-trees of the mountain attract his attention, and he points to them that he may teach the watchcare of Providence : "Are not five sparrows sold for two farthings, and not one of them is forgotten before God ? Fear not therefore : ye are of more value than many sparrows." Luke xii, 6, 7. Then another flock of birds attracts his attention, and he uses them to still further enforce this thought of God's care : "Consider the ravens : for they neither sow nor reap ; which neither have storehouse nor barn ; and God feedeth them : how much more are ye better than the fowls ?" Luke xii, 24. Then he weaves the vines and trees, and also the thistles and thorns, of the mountain into a lesson of diligence in showing faith by works : "Ye shall know them by their fruits. Do men gather grapes of thorns or figs of thistles ?" The cloud that appears in sight also bears him a message : "And he said, When ye see a cloud

---

* We use the familiar explanation of the "needle's eye," although there is a division of opinion between this explanation and others.

2

rise out of the west, straightway ye say, There cometh a shower; and so it is. Ye hypocrites, ye can discern the face of the sky and of the earth; but how is it that ye do not discern this time?"—the spiritual truth of my mission. Best of all, he impressed the lesson of God's personal watchcare, which he had taught by the sparrows and ravens, by turning to the beautiful white lilies of Palestine that bloomed abundantly about him, and saying: *Consider* the lilies; observe them carefully; take their lesson to heart; read it over and over. Consider the lilies: how abundantly they grow, how prosperously they grow, how mysteriously they grow. Consider the beauty of the lilies: Solomon in all the glory of his royal white robe was not arrayed with such beauty as this snowy lily. Wherefore, if God so *adorn* the grass and flowers of the field, which quickly fade, and are cast with the dry straw and withered herbs and stubble into the oven for fuel, how much more will he clothe you, O ye of little faith! The sparrows are almost worthless, and yet God watches over their *lives;* the ravens have no storehouse, yet our Father provides their *food;* the lilies toil not, and yet the Father gives them *raiment.* And shall not He who takes such care of the fowls in his yard and the plants in his garden much more clothe and care for you, who are the children of his fireside?

As the sibyl wrote her prophecies on leaves, so Jesus has written his truth on the lily blossom, the raven's wing, the ruby grape, the white grain, the passing cloud, the narrow and wide gates, the city of the hill-top, the water of the wayside well, and the fruit of the orchard. The Indians have a legend, mentioned in Hiawatha, that—

> " All the wild flowers of the forest,
> All the lilies of the prairie,
> When on earth they fade and perish,
> Blossom in the rainbow o'er us:
> 'Tis the heaven of flowers you see there."

Christ, on the other hand, took the heavenly rainbow of truth and put it into the " wild flowers " and " lilies " of earth.

Sandalphon, the angel of prayer, says the legend,

> "Gathers our prayers as he stands,
> And they turn into flowers in his hands."

The great Teacher shows us how we may take the flowers in our hands and *turn them into prayers.*

Were it necessary, it might be interesting to show in this connection how the Tabernacle was a great school for object-lessons, each part of it teaching the people a word of high import. As the child in his primer sees the *picture* of a house, and learns the *word* "House" below it the more readily, so God showed the people a bloody altar, and wrote under it that great word, "Atonement;" he showed them a laver of pure water, and taught them the word "Purity;" he showed them a golden candlestick, and taught them "Light;" the lamb was a prophecy of "the Lamb of God;" the vail, of Christ's flesh. God was teaching the unseen and eternal by the seen and temporal. These altars and lavers, etc., were but "*figures* of the true." The whole book of Hebrews teaches through these object-lessons. Christ himself was not only a sacrifice for us, but was also a grand visible lesson, illustrating to man how the characteristics of his God could be "made *manifest* in the flesh." God gave to men this privilege of seeing Christ in answer to that feeling that made it the intensest longing of the prophets and sweetest memory of the apostles to "see Jesus." The world desired to "*behold* the Lamb," unsatisfied, like Simeon, until it had "*seen* God's salvation." The Bible is the greatest text-book and store-house of object-lessons in the world. Every sacrifice and feast of the Old Testament, and every sacrament of the New, is an object-lesson. The Sabbath is an object-lesson of creation, and also of heaven ; the rainbow after the flood, the moving pillar in the wilderness, and every vision of prophecy, are object-lessons.

EYE-TEACHING ADAPTED TO THE TIMES.

We need only to refer to the increased amount of black-board work in our day-schools, to the large number of magazines and papers that have recently introduced illustrations into their heretofore unillustrated pages, to the inscriptions on rocks and fences, the great number of picture advertisements in our papers, and the increasing custom of illustrating lectures, to remind our readers that one marked characteristic of this age is an inclination to put things into the mind by a quick concentration on the eye. We must " discern the signs of the times " and keep up with them. We must study times and men. The advertising pages, which are epitomized photographs of the day, and the " Bitters " on stones, " Buchu " on trees, and " Magic Oil " on every thing, notwithstanding their quackery, teach us that this age must be reached very much through the eye.

With Whom should Eye-Teaching be Used?

Not with the little children alone by any means, nor with the ignorant simply. Christ used it in teaching the rich and wise Nicodemus. He taught him the greatest truth that man can ever learn by reminding him of the serpent lifted up in the wilderness, and using that as an object-lesson to teach him of redemption and regeneration. Paul was not too old or learned, after he had graduated from " the feet of Gamaliel," to be taught by an object-lesson. " As we tarried [at Cesarea] there many days, there came down from Judea a certain prophet, named Agabus. And when he was come unto us, he took Paul's girdle, and bound his own hands and feet, and said, Thus saith the Holy Ghost, So shall the Jews at Jerusalem bind the man that owneth this girdle." Acts xxi, 10, 11. God came to teach even the eloquent Peter, not exactly with outlines on a blackboard, but with " all manner of beasts in a sheet let down from heaven." The blackboard and object-lesson are as necessary in a school where there are many adults as in an infant-school. All feel the power of this God-given method of presenting the truth to the heart.

Who shall Conduct Eye-Teaching?

That which is to be given before the whole school should be conducted by the pastor, if he is the best man for such work, or by the superintendent, or by a selected teacher. Let the best workman be selected whatever his position. One may be best in object-teaching, another in blackboard work. In the latter not only skill in using chalk is to be considered, but also and especially ability to talk the subject sweetly into the hearts of those that hear. One may design the exercises and talk about them, having another who is a better artist to do the mechanical work. If there is an artist in the school, enlist his talent for Christ. " God sends us an artist, and he immediately becomes a blackboardist," said an enthusiastic Sunday-school pastor to a new member. And the artist recognized the Master's call to labor, and his heart answered, " Here am I, Lord ; " and from that hour the Sunday-school was the fortunate possessor of consecrated ability, displayed in the matter of exquisitely beautiful blackboard illustrations done in colored crayons. " He spends the whole of every Sunday afternoon in the exhaustive study of the lesson. When he has it *all by heart*, he makes a pencil sketch of the design of the picture that he means to furnish us with on the following Sunday. The first fresh hours of each morning of the week he gives to the work of drawing and coloring the large blackboard illustration so prized by our school ; and he adds the last loving, finishing touches to the whole on Sunday, just before bringing it up to the school."

Usually a simple outline sketch or word exercise would be better than such a picture, but if God gives you an artist, use him. Why not have a picture for the school on the blackboard as well as on the wall ? We cannot, however, emphasize too strongly the fact that object-lessons and blackboard exercises should, as a rule, be very simple, lest the *means* by which we teach shall draw the attention from the *truth* to be taught. When Moses and Elias, on the Mount of Transfiguration, divided and diverted the attention of the apostles from Christ, they were removed from sight, and the apostles "saw no man save Jesus only." Let the object-lessons vanish if they divert the eye from Jesus; let the blackboard fall, like Peter, James, and John, to the ground, if it stands between the scholars' hearts and Christ. Amid all these helps let the Sunday-school "hear Him" above all other voices.

What shall Give us Themes for Eye-Teaching?

Three things should usually have weight in selecting a map, story, or object-lesson, or in making a blackboard exercise: 1. The lesson of the school or class; 2. The events of the day; 3. The time of the year. While the lesson should usually be the center of the eye-teaching, yet, at times, striking and special events of the day or the season of the year may suggest other themes that will be impressive. If there is a temperance excitement, exercises on temperance might for a day be better than an exercise on the subject of the lesson. So in time of flowers, fruits, or autumn leaves, the season rather than the lesson may give the eye-teacher his theme.

Divisions of Eye-Teaching.

Taking the subject in a comprehensive view, we make the following divisions:

I. Vivid Description and Allegories.
II. Stories Vividly Told.
III. Stories Represented.
IV. Religious Object-Teaching.
V. Map-Teaching.
VI. Picture-Teaching.
VII. Blackboard Exercises.
  1. Motto Exercise.
  2. Topic Exercise.
  3. Initial Exercise.
  4. Syllable Exercise.
  5. Word Exercise.
  6. Phrase Exercise.
  7. Table Exercise.
  8. Acrostic Exercise.
  9. Parallel and Contrast Exercise.
  10. Canceling Exercise.
  11. Erasing Exercise.
  12. Word-Symbol Exercise.
  13. Map Exercise.
  14. Outline Exercise.

I. VIVID DESCRIPTION AND ALLEGORIES.

The scenes of the Bible, if vividly described from a thorough knowledge and sympathy with the circumstances, form a picture, a drama, that may properly be classed as eye-teaching. If the teacher is talking about Paul on Mars' Hill, let the surrounding scenes be so described that the scholar can put himself in Paul's place and make the scene real. Let the doctrines of the Epicureans and Stoics be so distinctly described that the application of every sentence shall be felt. If the Good Samaritan be the subject, let the teachers make the scholars feel the very shadow of the rocks on that dangerous way, and the moisture of the cloth with which the blood is wiped from the arms of the man left half dead. The Epistle to the Corinthians may be made as beautiful to the eye as a temple by a thorough understanding of the architecture of Ephesus, *from* which Paul wrote, and of Corinth, *to* which he wrote.

In fact, whatever the lesson may be, if all the geographical and historical knowledge connected with it is clustered around it there will be a picturesqueness and vividness that will add greatly to its power. Take the following illustration of this kind of description on the subject of FEEDING THE MULTITUDE:

The incident has its lesson for the pews as well as its encouragement for the pulpit. Christ might have scattered this heavenly manna, as of old, by the same miraculous power that multiplied it. He chose rather to use human agency, and "gave it to the disciples, and they gave it to the multitude." There was a great variety of tastes, talents, and dispositions among the disciples; but Christ used them all, not merely to distribute the bread, but also to impress its lesson. There was the loving John, the impulsive Peter, the doubting Thomas, the systematic Matthew, the law-loving James, and the others, each with some trait of character peculiarly his own. Sometimes, as I have thought of this incident, I have imagined the different feelings with which the disciples received the bread and thought of the miracle. John, as he took the loaves, would stand and look with his deep, loving eyes upon Jesus, almost forgetting the multitude as he gazed, "lost in wonder, love, and praise," upon his Master. Impulsive Peter would seize the loaves eagerly and hurry about, scattering them hastily among the multitude, and, with his emphasis and love of prophecy, proclaiming on every hand that they saw the promise fulfilled, "He shall feed his flock like a shepherd." James, with his love of the old law, would remind the people, as he scattered the bread, that the same power that fed their fathers in the wilderness was feeding them on the shores of Galilee. Systematic Matthew would remind the people how greatly the loaves had been multiplied and how many had been fed; while Thomas, as he took the bread from Jesus, would press his thumbs into the loaves that he might be assured he was not dreaming, and that he did not hold a phantom in his hand, meanwhile glancing cautiously at the Master, and whispering to his nearest friend, "What manner of man is this?"

Christ used all these various talents to get the bread and its lesson to the multitude; and so to-day the bread which is given to you with Christ's blessing from the written Word, the Spirit, and the Gospel ministry, God expects you to scatter among the multitude in your daily walks, around your firesides, along your waysides, and in your places of business.

"Give ye them to eat."

The sermons of Rev. T. De Witt Talmage abound in examples of vivid description of Bible scenes, and may profitably be studied by teachers as models in this respect.

The plan of representing abstract truths in concrete forms, and personifying the ideal, so beautifully illustrated by the parables of our Lord, and also by the fables of Æsop and the allegories of Bunyan and others, may often be used to great advantage by the Sunday-school teacher. Dr. Eggleston once told a company of children of a house that a king had built with two beautiful windows, two wonderful servants, etc., to which that king sent his son, and the man who lived in the king's house refused to let him in; in short, making the human body and soul an allegorical house, and describing it in such a way that the children could surmise, before he finished the description, that he was talking of them and Christ's coming for admittance to their hearts.

GIFTS FROM A CASKET.—[This exercise, contributed by Rev. W. E. Huntington, shows very well how abstract truth may be presented in an attractive verbal form.] A speaker addressing a body of children desires to talk of some of the virtues and graces that should adorn character. Let him tell the children he has some gifts to distribute to them. He has a ring for each finger on both hands. Then, holding up the first finger of his left hand, let him call the ring for that finger Obedience, for example, and ask the children to repeat the word in unison. A story may be told illustrative of this virtue. And so on for each finger of both hands. This list may be used for the rings: Obedience, Truthfulness, Courtesy, Kindness, Cheerfulness, Humility, Temperance, Love. Calling these virtues rings, and slipping them upon their fingers, in imagination, will prove to be the best way of fastening the lessons to be taught upon the memories of children. Their attention may be held more closely by frequently asking them to repeat the names of the rings in concert, following the order in which they have been given. Then, as they will want to show these gifts to their friends, they must have sandals upon their feet. Call these sandals Courage. Let them repeat this word in a full, clear voice. Show how without these sandals it would be useless to try to wear some of the rings—Obedience and Temperance, for instance. Then give them a girdle of Christlikeness, showing how, as a girdle binds the garments closely about one, that he may run or work well, so Christlikeness is a comprehensive quality of character that will enable us to live well. Lastly, place the crown of Faith upon their heads. Speak of faith as the highest ornament of character. It links us to God, and therefore ought to be placed above all others, as a crowning grace. Then let the names of the rings, of the sandals, of the girdle, of the crown, be repeated in concert, and the speaker may close by telling his audience of little hearers that these ornaments are of finer stuff than silver or gold, and will not wear out nor tarnish by wearing them every day, but will only grow brighter by use, and that they come from God's casket of jewels—the Bible.*

II.—STORIES VIVIDLY TOLD.

The great teachers of the race are those who have clothed truth in stories of some kind. Æsop, Bunyan, Beecher, Spurgeon, and a host of others, are examples of this class. A man gave to Christ, as he thought, a troublesome question, "Who is my neighbor?" It was answered vividly with the story of the good Samaritan.

Jews regarded with scorn the "publicans and sinners" that had accepted Christ. Jesus taught them their duty by the prodigal's story. Ralph Wells writes: "I asked a young woman upon the street, 'What portion of the Scripture did you the most good?' She replied, 'That which does all men good, the parable of the prodigal son. It is so pleasant, so plain! There stands the father with outstretched arms. It is wonderful, the love of Jesus Christ for the sinner!'" Stories vividly told, put on as a garment, are a part of eye-teaching. The teacher should be amply supplied with them. "Where will you go to-day?" said a mother to her little

---

* The author has heard the writer of the above form a group of allegorical statuary of the virtues: Valor, as a true soldier, first set up, and then Knowledge, as a true scholar; Temperance, as a man of strength and health and manliness; and so, following with Patience, Brotherly-Kindness, Faith, and Love, making them seem like a group of statues upon the platform around him as he described their characteristics, and giving some incident illustrative of each one after describing it

girl, " to Aunt Mary's or Aunt Jane's?" She replied, "I will go to see Aunt Jane, for she always has plenty of ginger snaps and keeps them on the lowest shelf." The teacher should have plenty of stories and " keep them on the lowest shelf," so that children can understand them; a note-book and pencil always with him and a scrap-book at home will easily gather the " snaps."

This is good advice from a teacher: " Use the pencil. It is easy to carry. It aids the memory. It catches and keeps a thousand flitting thoughts. Carry a small blank book. If you see a fact or think a thought that may be of any possible use in the future take note of it. You may not *now* see of what service it can be, but when interested in a lesson you may glance over the penciled jottings and find one, two, ten helpful illustrations or allusions, the worth of which, in the exposition of your subject, may be invaluable. One fact a day thus taken into captivity will register three hundred and sixty-five a year—so many servitors in your work. Use the pencil."

Henry Clay Trumbull writes these excellent words about telling Bible stories vividly: " It has been urged by some earnest Sunday-school writer that children should never be trapped into hearing a Bible story, by its recital in homely language, as if it were from another source than the Book of God. But there are two sides to even that question. If a child is disinclined to hear Bible stories, it is not fair to assume you are telling him something else when he is sure to find at the close that you have palmed off one of the obnoxious narratives in another garb. On the other hand, it is eminently desirable to so clothe the Bible history to children as to give to the persons and incidents thereof a naturalness and reality that is not secured to little folks through the somewhat obsolete forms of our common English version. What would be wrong for purposes of deception is quite proper for the purpose of elucidation.

" An incident in my own experience confirms my opinion on this point. I well recall the time when I had far more reverence for than understanding of the Bible. Scripture characters were to me not only mythical but unintelligible. The difference between Genesis and Euroclydon was by no means clear to my mind. I did not know who Deuteronomy was, nor what was Jehoshaphat. The first dawn of clear day came in this way. My home was by the sea-side, where figures of sailor life were familiar to all. One afternoon a good man came to our Sabbath-school gathering, and, entering the desk by request of the superintendent, commenced to tell a story. He described a sea-shore scene, with a vessel in the offing weighing anchor and loosing sail for a voyage. Vividly, in word painting, he showed a boat putting off from the dock, bringing at the last moment a passenger for the trip, his clambering on to the dock, the start of the vessel, its progress, a gathering storm, danger on the deep, the fright of passengers and crew, a consultation, and the confession of the late-coming passenger that he was a fugitive pursued of God for his sin, hence the storm and the peril to all. O how well I remember the new light that burst into my mind when I then recognized the hitherto unreal story of Jonah as a living verity! I felt as did the boy who at last saw Lafayette through the carriage window, and called out in amazement, ' Why, he's only a *man !* ' ' Jonah ' had been *Jonah* to me until that hour. Now he was a *man.* ' Joppa ' had been *Joppa.* Now it was a *sea-port town.* My little brain was almost bewildered with the discovery that the Bible had something in it that I could understand ; but the vail of mystery that had enwrapped it until then went overboard with Jonah when that Sunday-school speaker had him thrown into the sea in the story. The entrance of God's words gave me light just as soon as those words were so stated that they could enter my child-mind. I am confident that I should not have been so profited at that time had the narrator announced in commencing that he was to tell us a Bible story. His course may, I think, be safely commended to many a teacher of the young.

"At the Newsboys' Lodging House in New York, ten years ago, I heard Mr. Tracy, the then Superintendent, entrap, as some might call it, his motley audience into hearing a Bible story when they would not have listened quietly to his reverent reading of the sacred narrative. Commencing the parable of the prodigal son, he told it in what would have seemed slang phrase to others, but in language which was really the vernacular of those boys. He held their fixed attention as he proceeded, and when their interest was most intense he said suddenly:

" But, boys, this story is all written out in a book I have here. Let me read you the rest of it.' And he opened the Bible and continued the narration, reading and explaining or translating by turn. Who shall say he was irreverent, or caused his hearers to be? "

III.—STORIES REPRESENTED.

Stories that are read may sometimes be a little vivified by using or showing something mentioned in the story. In telling the story of Joseph when he sent the message to Jacob, a piece of brown paper (which will represent parchment) may be cut into a foot square and rolled up as a Jewish scroll, with this letter written upon it, to be read after the scroll is described and the circumstances narrated—Gen. xlv, 9, etc.:

EGYPT, 1706.

JACOB ISRAEL,—Thus saith thy son Joseph: I am yet alive. Come down to me; tarry not; and thou shalt be near to me, and I will nourish thee.

JOSEPH, *Lord of all Egypt.*

This letter should be written with the lines slanting very much, as the slant in Jewish letters indicates love.

With this story of Joseph the passage from Revelation may be read : "Fear not : I am he that liveth and was dead, and behold, I am alive for evermore." This may be used to show that Joseph was not dead, although unseen ; so Christ is not dead, but "ever lives above." Other analogies may also be brought out—for example, the Lord is our Shepherd, and has also become a King, and we "shall not want."

CHILDLIKE CHRISTIANITY.—Another opportunity for this kind of teaching is afforded by Matt. xviii, 1–6. Superintendent Whittles, of New York, once took a child in his arms before the school, and read the verses above, and explained them, with the child itself as a living illustration that "in malice" we are to be children, and also in faith, trust, innocence, and love.

THE SAW OF CONTENTION.—Show a small saw ; or the outline of a saw may be drawn upon the blackboard, marked, "The Saw of Contention." Illustrate by the following :

"O Frank ! come and see how hot my saw gets when I rub it. When I draw it through the board awhile it's 'most hot enough to set fire to it."

"That's the friction," said Frank, with all the superior wisdom of two years more than Eddie boasted.

"Yes," said Sister Mary, who was passing ; "it's the friction ; but do you know what it makes me think of ?"

"No, what ?" asked both the boys at once.

"Of two little boys who were quarreling over a trifle this morning, and the more they talked the hotter their tempers grew, until there was no knowing what might have happened if mother had not thrown cold water on the fire by sending them into separate rooms."

The boys hung their heads, and Mary went on :

"There is an old proverb which says, 'The longer the saw of contention is drawn the hotter it grows.'"

"I tell you what, Frank," said Eddie, " when we find ourselves getting angry, let's run out and use the saw Kriss

Kringle brought me, and then we wont find time for the saw of contention."

"THE PAST ALL UNDER THE BLOOD."—Another illustration of this class:—Take three pieces of muslin or paper, one black, another blood-red, and another white, and cut them into three leaves of equal size. Put them into some small blank-book cover, and fasten them in so that the first leaf shall be black, the next red, the next white. Use it in telling and applying this incident. An old preacher was accustomed to walk often in his garden with a little book in his hand. His friends wondered what there was about the book that made it so interesting. They found it had but three leaves, and nothing written or printed on either of them, yet his face changed from sadness to joy as he turned it over. The first page was perfectly black, [show it,] the next red, [show it,] the next white [show it.] At length he told them its meaning. The black represented the guilty and sorrowful days of his sin, and no black was deep enough to represent it; the red reminded him of the cleansing blood, and the white, of his heart cleansed by the blood. Notice especially that when you turn the second page the black is all *under the red,* so when the atonement is applied to our hearts "*the past is all under the blood.*" "Though your sins be as scarlet, they shall be white as snow."

The following story may also be used in this way, having a flower in the hand, that the "delicate veins" and "branches," and other points, may be shown at the appropriate time

THE ATHEIST AND THE FLOWER. — When Napoleon Bonaparte was Emperor of France, he put a man by the name of Charney into prison. He thought Charney was an enemy of his government, and for that reason deprived him of his liberty. Charney was a learned and profound man, and as he walked to and fro in the small yard into which his prison opened he looked up to the heavens the work of God's fingers, and to the moon and stars which he ordained, and exclaimed, "All things come by chance!"

One day, while pacing his yard, he saw a tiny plant just breaking the ground near the wall. The sight of it caused a pleasant diversion of his thoughts. No other green thing was within his inclosure. He watched its growth every day. "How came it here?" was his natural inquiry. As it grew other queries were suggested. "How came these delicate little veins in its leaves? What made its proportions so perfect in every part, each new branch taking its exact place on the parent stock, neither too near another, nor too much on one side?"

In his loneliness the plant became the prisoner's teacher and his valued friend. When the flower began to unfold he was filled with delight. It was white, purple, and rose-colored, with a fine silvery fringe. Charney made a frame to support it, and did what his circumstances allowed to shelter it from pelting rains and violent winds.

"All things come by chance," had been written by him upon the wall, just above where the flower grew. Its gentle reproof as it whispered, "There is One who made me so wonderfully beautiful, and he it is who keeps me alive," shamed the proud man's unbelief. He brushed the lying words from the wall, while his heart felt that "He who made all things is God."

But God had a further blessing for the erring man through the humble flower. There was an Italian prisoner in the same yard whose little daughter was permitted to visit him. The girl was much pleased with Charney's love for his flower. She related what she saw to the wife of the jailer. The story of the prisoner and his flower passed from one to another, until it reached the ears of the amiable Empress Josephine. The Empress said, "The man who so devotedly loves and tends a flower cannot be a bad man," so she persuaded the Emperor to set him at liberty. Thus the

flower was to him like the angel that visited Peter's prison—
his deliverer from the chains of his body and his soul.
Charney carried his flower home, and carefully tended it in
his own green-house. It had taught him to believe in a
God, and had delivered him from prison.

> "All things bright and beautiful
> All creatures, great and small,
> All things wise and wonderful,
> The Lord God made them all."

"HE DIED FOR ME."—Make on the black-board the simple
outline of a grave-stone and a grave. On the stone (really
board, as the story shows, but it would appear the same as
stone) write "HE DIED FOR ME." Tell the following
story, and apply it to Christ's death for us:

In the cemetery at Nashville, Tennessee, a stranger was
seen planting a flower over a soldier's grave. When asked,
"Was your son buried there?"

"No," was the answer.

"Your son-in-law?" "No."

"A brother?" "No."

"A relative?" "No."

After a moment the stranger laid down a small board
which he held in his hand, and said:

"Well, I will tell you. When the war broke out I was
a farmer. I wanted to enlist, but I was poor, and had a wife
and seven young children. I was drafted, had no money to
hire a substitute, and so I made up my mind that I must
leave my poor sickly wife and little children, and go and
serve in the army. After I had got ready to go a young
man whom I knew came to me and said, 'You have a big
family, which your wife cannot take care of. I will go for
you.' He did go in my place, and in the battle of Chicka-
mauga he was wounded, and taken to Nashville hospital.
After a long sickness he died, and was buried here; and
ever since I have wanted to come to Nashville and see his

grave; and so I saved up all the spare money I could, and yesterday I came on, and to-day I found my dear friend's grave."

With tears of gratitude running down his cheeks, he took up the small board and pressed it down into the ground in the place of a tombstone. Under the soldier's name were written these words: "HE DIED FOR ME.

THE BIBLE.—Tell the following story, with a Bible at hand to show at the appropriate time. After the story explain how the Bible fulfills the dream:

Mary was sleeping. An angel came and laid under her hand a beautiful book. Then he said softly, "This is the lamp to guide you in darkness, the curtain to cover you from danger, the word of promise to keep you safely while you sleep, and the sweet voice to talk with you when you are awake." Then the angel kissed her, and sped away on his wings of light to his home beyond the stars. Mary awoke. It was only a dream, yet it seemed as if an angel had really talked with her in her sleep; and ever since she has loved [taking up the Bible] her precious Bible as the word of God more than ever she loved it before, for the "beautiful book" which the angel laid under her hand was the Bible, and it is indeed a "guide," a "curtain," a protector, and a "sweet voice" to cheer us.

THE KEY OF HEAVEN. — Making on the black-board a number of keys large enough to receive the inscriptions indicated in the story below, or taking a bunch of keys in the hand to use as an object-lesson, the following popular allegory, by Dr. Vincent, can be visibly illustrated:

I had a vision of the Holy City. Its walls rose before me strong and lofty, resplendent with the glory of amethyst and jacynth, of jasper and sapphire. The gate before which I stood was of "one pearl," and it shone with variegated colors—crimson and emerald, violet and orange. I noticed upon this gate a beautiful band and cross-band of pure and shining white, forming a cross as lofty and with arms as broad as the gate itself. Over the city hung a dome of golden light, throbbing ever and anon with fresh splendor, as though some new glory had been unfolded before the throne, and its reflection had been thrown upward from "the sea of glass mingled with fire."

"That is the light they love," said my angel guide.

Bursts of music, blending the softest notes of melody with the loudest thunders, greeted my ear. It was as though all the voices of the universe joined in a chorus of praise.

"These," said my guide, "are the songs they sing."

The atmosphere seemed burdened with the most fragrant odors, at once delicate, delicious, and exhilarating, so that, inhaling it, I was endowed with a double force of life.

As the gate of the city opened I saw within. The inner glory dazzled my eyes. Shading them with my hand, that I might catch a glimpse of this wonderful world, I saw trooping forth through the open gate a numberless multitude of children, leaping and singing in very excess of joy. So fair a picture I had never seen. The faces of the little ones were radiant. Their voices rang out in sweetest song. Then my guide said to me, "These are the little ones so dearly loved on earth, early removed from their earthly homes and made the children of heaven. They, with their guardian angels, do always behold the face of their Father in heaven."

Then the gate closed.

I also sought to enter the Holy City.

"Hast thou the key?" inquired my guide.

I answered, "I have no key."

"There are many keys brought to this gate by which men seek to enter. Only one can turn the bolt. Alas, that so few bring it! Alas, that so few out of the multitudes that seek ever enter this beautiful portal!"

"Show me the cause of it, and give me the true key," I said.

" Look !"

Then I saw a company of men and women from the earth drawing nigh unto the glorious gate. As they paused for a time, scarcely knowing what next to do, or how to approach the shining portal, my guide led me to them and said, " Inspect the keys they bear." As the pilgrims were nothing loth to let me see what they held, I was able to examine many of the keys. On one I found the simple word " Reward." On another this inscription, " Rest." One read " Reunion," and the fourth, " Knowledge." Some bore the word "Happiness."

"These," said my guide, " are specimens of the keys that most men carry up to the gates of heaven." So saying he bade the company proceed.

Now I noticed, and with much surprise, that these keys all failed to turn the bolt; and the look of disappointment on the faces of the rejected threw on the gate itself a deep and dismal shadow.

"You see," said my guide, " that these expected heaven as a ' reward ' for labor performed, or as a ' rest ' from labor, or as a place of ' reunion' with departed friends much loved, long lost. Others of them sought it through an almost idle curiosity, expecting that in heaven all problems would be solved and their knowledge increased ; while all reputed ' happiness ' the thing most to be desired and sought after by an immortal soul."

' But does not God's word," I asked, " promise all these— rest, reward, reunion, knowledge, and happiness ?

" Very true," said the angel, " but merely as incidentals, not as essentials. The life and delight of heaven are not in these."

" Who, then, can enter ? " I inquired anxiously.

Just then I saw one come to the gate, key in hand. Scarcely had his key touched the gate when it opened widely, and the stranger stepped forward into the midst of the un-vailed and dazzling glory of the opened gate.

Then the angel showed me the mystic key—the key of heaven. On the face of it I read the word JESUS, and on the stem I read the words WITH HIM—LIKE HIM, and on the handle of it SEE HIM—SERVE HIM.

So I learned that the *love* of Jesus, and the *longing after* Jesus, and *likeness* to Jesus constitute the true life and de-light of heaven; that they alone are prepared for heaven who find in Christ their richest joy, who seek the gate be-cause he is beyond it, who press toward the throne because he is upon it. And I learned, moreover, that to all besides these the heaven of the Bible is but an idle dream, and will be a disappointment.

Dear Sunday-school teacher, seek for the true love of Jesus Christ; fix the thought and love of your scholars upon him; find him in all the lessons of the Word; leave him with your class as the last thought and the best thought of every recitation, and thus hold in your own hand, and place in the hands of your pupils, the one only key that can open the gate of pearl to an immortal soul.

"I'LL NEVER FORGET THEE."—There is a legend which ac-counts for the name of the forget-me-not, which may be told with the flower in the hand:

It is said that two lovers were walking by the side of a river, when, by some mishap, the man's foot slipped and he fell into the water. As he could not swim, he sank once and again. There was no rope, or board, or boat by which the lady could help him, and she stood on the bank frantically wringing her hands. No other person was near enough to hear his cries for "Help!" As he was about to sink for the last time he looked toward the lady and threw a flower, which he still held in his hand, to her feet, saying, "Forget me not." Hav-ing had such a christening, the name has ever remained with the flower. Apply the story as follows:—So in early days

man walked with God in the garden, but by sin and disobedience man was separated from God, and was "far off by
wicked works;" but God threw back the flowers in rich abun-
dance at our feet, and cried, "Forget me not," and so I call
all the flowers *God's forget-me-nots.*

Taking a strawberry plant, illustrate this thought still
further with the following story, showing briefly some of the
wonders of its leaves and stems and fruit:

THE NEARNESS OF GOD.—A missionary visited a poor old
woman living alone in a city attic, and whose scanty pittance
of half a crown a week was scarcely sufficient for her bare
subsistence. He observed in a broken tea-pot that stood at
the window a strawberry plant growing. He remarked
from time to time how it continued to grow, and with what
care it was watched and tended. One day he said, "Your
plant flourishes nicely; you will soon have strawberries upon
it." "O, sir," replied the woman, "it is not for the sake of
the fruit that I prize it, but I am too poor to keep any living
creature, and it is a great comfort to me to have that living
plant, for I know it can only live by the power of God; and
as I see it live and grow from day to day, it tells me that
God is near."

THE FATAL HOUR.—An ocean steamer went down with all
on board. A clock washed ashore which had stopped at
eleven o'clock, showing the hour when the vessel sank. This
story can be told, and then, looking to a clock or watch, the
moment may be noted, with the remark, "Perhaps at this
moment some one of you is deciding the question of your
whole eternity."

CONSCIENCE.—Draw the outline of an old-fashioned clock
on the board, and tell the following story:
Little Charley was one Sabbath left at home alone by his
father and mother. They told him not to touch the old tall

clock in the parlor, but to read his library book and remember it was Sunday. When he had read his book all through it was so still that he could hear the old clock in the other room—"Tick, tick, tick." He thought some one must be talking in there, and peeped in through the door. Then it seemed as if the talking came from inside the clock—"Tick tick, tick." He started to see about it, and then he remembered that mother had told him not to touch the clock. But he said, "I'll just peep in, and mother never will know it." He opened the door and touched the swinging pendulum with his hand. It stopped, and he was frightened. No more "Tick, tick." When mother came she asked him if he had touched the clock, and he said, "No." He felt very sad when he went to bed, and was afraid to go to sleep. Father had fixed the clock, and very soon he heard it, not saying "Tick, tick, tick," but this was what he thought he heard— "Lie-lie, lie-lie, lie-lie." He put a pillow over his head to keep out the sound. Soon he heard it again a little lower— "Lie-lie, lie-lie." He put the other pillow over his head. But soon he heard again, "Lie-lie, lie-lie." Then he said to himself, "I have done wrong; I disobeyed mother, and I lied." After a little he went down and knelt at mother's knee, and asked her to forgive him and to pray that God would forgive him. When he got up from his knees he was happy, and went up to his little bed singing with joy. He lay down, and very soon he heard the old clock again, and this was what it said, "Truth-truth, truth-truth." It seemed almost to sing until he went to sleep. So, dear little folks, if you do wrong it will make you very sad; and if you do right it will make you very happy.

Still another exercise of this class is the

TAYLOR JUG.—Take such a jug as is ordinarily used for strong drink, and break the bottom out; then use it with this story: Dr. Tyng met an emigrant family going West. On one of the wagons there hung a jug, with the bottom knocked out. "What is that?" asked the doctor. "Why, it is my Taylor jug," said the man. "And what is a Taylor jug?" asked the doctor again. "I had a son in General Taylor's army in Mexico, and the General always told him to carry his whisky jug with a hole in the bottom; and that's it. It is the best invention I ever met with for hard drinkers."

The stories of the Bible can often be told with some Eastern or missionary relic to illustrate them, or something resembling objects mentioned in the accounts: the parable of the vineyard with a bunch of grapes, Joseph's dream with a handful of wheat, Stephen's death with a pile of stones, Joseph sold for twenty pieces of silver with a handful of coin, the tribute money scene with a piece of money, etc. A preacher, in speaking about the heathen, took a heathen god from his pocket and intensified his words by bringing the simple object into his story at the right time.*

IV.—RELIGIOUS OBJECT-TEACHING.

We shall try to answer five questions that are often asked in regard to object-teaching in the Sunday-school: 1. *What* is religious object-teaching? 2. *Why* should it be used? 3. *When* should it be used? 4. *Where* shall we obtain objects? and, 5. *How* shall we use them?

What is religious object-teaching? We can most readily show what it is by comparing it with the well-known object-teaching of our best day-schools.

In the day-school an object is presented to the eye—a leaf, a flower, a mineral, a fossil, or a bone—to be studied for its own sake, and the lesson is perfect only when every quality

---

* Rev. J. S. Ostrander has prepared a box of " Oriental Block Models " that enable the teacher to give at once a cheap, accurate, and vivid representation, in their real forms, of the tabernacle, temple, Jewish house, wine-press, and other specimens of Bible architecture. Any part of the Bible that has architectural references may be most effectively illustrated by this ingenious arrangement.

and attribute of the object is known. In the Sunday-school, on the other hand, the object, although it may be any of those mentioned above, is studied as a symbol, a suggestion, a picture of some thought or idea far above itself, and the lesson is perfect when the attention is secured by the object, and the one or two qualities that may illustrate the thought which is being presented are understood.

We may illustrate the day-school object-teaching by a recitation at DOTHEBOY'S HALL:

"'This is the first class in English spelling and philosophy, Nickleby,' said Squeers, beckoning Nicholas to stand beside him. 'Now, then, where's the first boy?'

"'Please, sir, he's cleaning the back parlor window,' said the temporary head of the philosophical class.

"'So he is, to be sure,' rejoined Squeers. 'We go upon the practical mode of teaching, Nickleby; the regular education system: c-l-e-a-n, clean, verb active, to make bright, to scour. W-i-n, win, d-e-r, der, winder, a casement. When the boy knows this out of a book he goes and does it. It's just the same principle as the use of the globes. Where's the second boy?'

"'Please, sir, he's weeding the garden,' replied a small voice.

"'To be sure,' said Squeers, by no means disconcerted. 'So he is. B-o-t, bot, t-i-n, tin, bottin, n-e-y, ney, bottinney, noun substantive, a knowledge of plants. When he has learned that bottinney means a knowledge of plants he goes and knows 'em. That's our system, Nickleby.'"

Although we should hardly give this as a model lesson, yet it illustrates the great characteristics of object-teaching in day-schools. The lesson is perfect when all the qualities of the weeds and the "winder" are ascertained. When the scholar "goes and knows 'em" they lead to nothing further. Religious object-teaching would lead us to look through the "winder" to something greater beyond; it would point us below the roots and above the blossoms of the plants to the Hand that made them.

The following will exactly illustrate the point we have just mentioned. A boy brought home to his father the teacher's report of his standing, which proved to be much below his usual mark. The father asked him why it was, and he replied that he .didn't know. The father knew, however, for he had noticed yellow-covered novels lying about the house during the few days previous. He turned to his son and said, "Empty that basket full of apples upon the floor, and then go out and fill the basket half full of chips."

The son, not suspecting any thing, obeyed. When he had brought the basket half full of chips the father said, "Now put back those apples into the basket." After half of them had been put in they began to roll off. "Put them all in; put them in," said the father sternly.

"I cannot," was the reply.

"Of course you cannot," said the father. "You said you did not know why you had fallen off in standing. Of course, you cannot fill your mind with useful knowledge after getting it half full of that yellow-covered trash you have been reading."

The boy blushed and went away, but never afterward touched one of those novels. In this object-lesson it would have been a waste of time and an injury to the lesson to have had the boy notice any further qualities about chips than the fact that they occupied the room which belonged to more valuable articles. When the object shown in Sunday-school is so used as to make it more prominent than the truth to be taught, it is exalting a "chip" above a moral precept. As much as a flag is less than the loyalty it represents, so much less than the truth presented should the object appear. The highest quality of an object used in Sunday-school teaching is that it should be a perfect mirror, itself almost unnoticed, while reflecting some great idea.

I passed a calm, still lake one starlight night, and beneath its motionless surface there seemed to be "new heavens," the stars were so perfectly reflected in its watery depths, the evening star shining brightest of all. So the religious object-lesson should reflect heavenly things, the Star of Bethlehem always being most prominent in its teachings and suggestions.

2. *Why should object-teaching be used in the Sunday-school?* For the answer to this question the reader is referred to the first pages of this book.

3. *When should object-lessons be used?* (1.) Frequently, as the Saviour used them, lest they shall attract too much attention because of their novelty, and because almost every lesson may be made more interesting at some point by their use. (2.) Only when they may be introduced naturally to help the truth; never as a "side exhibition" attached to the truth rather than an incidental illustration of it.

The younger the scholars, the more frequently should object-lessons be used.

But, 4. *Where shall we get object-lessons?* Generally, not from the books and magazines. The model exercises given in institutes, books, and papers should be read for the suggestions and principles they contain, instead of being literally followed. David in Goliath's hat or Saul's armor would not be more awkward than a teacher often becomes in trying to use, without modification, the object-lesson of another.

The "How," not the "What," should be the question in our minds as we study the object-lessons of others.

For finding object-lessons "the field is the world." The good teacher transforms every phase of life into an illustration. As the delicate plate of the photographer catches a picture of whatever is before it, so the teacher who has put his mind into the illustrative mood catches illustrations from every passing event.

Briefly and rapidly it may be shown how fertile in object-lessons are the fields in which we all walk, how abundant are the lessons within "arm's length" of every day life. Sitting in my study this very afternoon, let me see how many object-lessons may be found without leaving the room: First, I will search myself. In my breast pocket I find *a letter* from one of our Sunday-school editors promising me a sum of money. The promise would be of no value unless it had a name I could trust signed to it. This letter, then, may be used as an object-lesson to show why we trust in the promises of the Bible : it is because the name of Jesus is signed to them.

In the same pocket is my Berean DAY-BOOK, with a space for every day in the year. The future days are blank, the past days not used as well as they should have been. This object will illustrate the Book of Remembrance, (see Outline Exercises.) In my vest pocket is a *watch*. It may be used as indicated in "Seed-Thought for Eye Teaching." From my pocket I take a *handful of coin*. It may be used to illustrate the story of Joseph sold into slavery, of Christ sold by Judas, or any other incident of Bible history where money is mentioned. On this *two cent piece* is the motto "In God we trust," a good object and text for a talk on God's care of our country. I take out my walllet. Here are some *railroad tickets*. The name of the superintendent signed to them gives me a passport from one place to another. So the name of Jesus gives us a passport to heaven.

This *counterfeit currency* and this *counterfeit bill* also suggest lessons. Sinful pleasure promises to pay us joy "six months after a treaty of peace" between our consciences and sin.

This *life insurance receipt* will illustrate the soul's insurance of heavenly life. Then, this *bunch of keys* is an excellent illustration of God's promises. Starting with the story of "The Key of Promise," I would say that every one of the promises is a key to lock in some treasure, or lock out some enemy, or unlock some store of heavenly wealth. This watch-key suggests the promise with which we "wind up" our trust every day, "As thy days so shall thy strength be." This trunk key represents the traveler's promise, "Lo, I am with you alway;" this house key, "Thou wilt keep him in perfect peace whose mind is stayed on thee;" this church

key, "They that wait on the Lord shall renew their strength."
This key to my post-office box may represent the promise of
prayer, by which we receive God's messages, "Whatsoever
ye shall ask in my name I will do it;" this safe key, (if I had
one,) "There is that scattereth and yet increaseth;" this
skeleton key that will unlock the church door, house door,
bed-room door, and many others, the promises that apply to
a great variety of cases: "The Lord will provide;" "My
grace is sufficient for thee." *My body* may be used as an
object-lesson of God's wisdom, for we are all "wonderfully
made;" or it may be used allegorically, as in Eccles. xii.

Turning now to my desk and its contents, this white paper
is an object-lesson, (see illustration in "Seed-Thought for
Object-Lessons.") This sheet of *red blotting paper* may il-
lustrate the promise of the "crimson made white as wool."
Formerly men could not whiten crimson rags; from them
therefore they must make paper of crimson or some other hue.
But Christ can make the crimson stain as white as snow.
Here is an *ink bottle* labeled "Ink," but the ink is no
longer there. So some persons bear the label "Christian"
when the Christlikeness has all disappeared. Here is my
Bible. It may be used as indicated in "Stories Represented."
My pocket looking-glass, which I have just taken from a
pigeon-hole, is cracked, and therefore makes a poor reflection,
as our professedly Christian hearts, when not right in the
sight of God, reflect Christ imperfectly. This *photograph*
of Abraham Lincoln may be used as indicated in the "Seed-
Thoughts for Object-Lessons."

These *four crackers*, one in the shape of a diamond, another
a cross, another a star, another a heart, given me by one of
my little friends, were too sacred to eat, and so here they are
in this pigeon-hole. In bringing them home the stamp of the
name was accidentally broken out of the cross, and the
heart, which had no name, was broken on one side. The
star and diamond crackers were perfect. Let me try to
get a sermon out of these by questioning my little friend,

Alice, who happens to be in my study for a few minutes this afternoon. What are these? "Crackers." What do you see on this star cracker? "Dots." What else? "Letters." What do you think the letters spell? "The name of the man that made it." When do you think the name was stamped on it—when it was soft, or after it was baked? "When it was soft." If they had tried to stamp it when it was hard, what would have happened? "They would break it." [Put the cracker out of sight.] Whose name ought we to have written on our hearts? "Jesus's." When ought it to be written there—when we grow old, or when we are children? "When we are children." When is it easiest to love God? "When we are children." The Bible says if we are good we shall shine as the stars. [Show star cracker.] Now repeat with me, "Shine as the stars for ever and ever." Now, you see this cross cracker looks bad because the name is broken out. We must never lose the name of Jesus from our hearts. And this heart cracker has no name. Could we stamp a name on it now? "No; it would break." How sad that any heart should not have a Jesus in it! Christ says that we shall be his in the day that he makes up his jewels. [Show diamond cracker.] Jesus loves those that he saves better than his crown or his throne. They are his jewels. [Incident of the mother of the Gracchi.]

Here beside my desk is a large *calla lily*. For its use see "Seed-Thought for Object-Lessons." In the vase with it are some apple blossoms. With them I can illustrate the fostering care of God over children, bringing them up to manhood But these are severed from the tree and are fading. I might use them to illustrate the fifteenth of John. Trailing over my bay window is an ivy which I might use with the same questions as the lesson on the Vine in "Seed-Thought for Object-Lessons." The plants in my hanging basket and flower pots can be used with the story of "The Atheist and the Flower" in "Stories Represented."

These pictures on my wall—"Bible Trees," Belshazzar's

Feast," "A Flower Scene," "The Key of Promise"—may be used for picture teaching; also, this portfolio of sacred pictures, cut from the illustrated papers of the day. I have not exhansted the list, but have said enough to show how abundant are the objects within reach of every teacher.

Toby Veck listened to the chimes' as to a living voice, and little Nell's friend heard whispers in the flames of his forge. Shakspeare heard Ariels in the breeze. To Byron "every mountain top had found a tongue." To Tennyson every tree is a "talking oak." To Longfellow, "the voiceless lips of flowers" are "living preachers." Whittier says that "such music as the woods and streams sang in his ear he sang aloud." The Sunday-school teacher needs this "open eye and ear," that every bell and flame and mountain-top and tree and flower and stream may be interpreted, and their God-sent messages understood. Like the servant of the prophet, if our eyes were opened we should see the mountains and fields full of the messages of God.

To the writers of the Bible the rolling year was full of object-lessons : seed, blooming flowers, harvests, withered leaves, "snow like morsels"—all these gave subjects for spiritual teaching. So relics of history, the serpent in the wilderness, the budding rod, the pillar of cloud and fire, the temple vessels, etc., gave them frequent object-lessons. They found in wayside walls, vineyards, kitchens, shops, and temples, some object on which they could hang the truth. Like them, the teacher should find in the garden, the fields, and the home, object-lessons for his work. For young scholars and infant departments especially objects are invaluable. There should be a box or drawer somewhere in connection with the school in which missionary relics, historic trophies, and any object that can be used as an object-lesson, may be kept, new ones being constantly added. And yet the best object-lessons will be those that are fresh and suggested by the present need.

5. *How shall object-lessons be prepared and taught?* In

answering this most important question there are three
suggestions for the preparation and four for the teaching:

PREPARATION: (1.) "Search the Scriptures" by means of
the Concordance and other helps for all the Scripture
passages that may in any way be connected with the object.

(2.) The attributes and uses of the object should be ascertained by a careful analysis. A teacher who fails to do this
may be embarrassed and surprised by unexpected develop-
ments at the time of teaching. A true story is told of a
Roman Catholic priest, who some years ago entered a pulpit
in Germany, carrying in his hand a walnut, his intention being to use it as an illustration of what he was about to say.
Holding up the little nut in full view of his crowded audience, he began, in a loud and boasting tone, with, "My
hearers, the shell of this nut is tasteless and valueless: that,
my friends, was Calvin's Church. The skin of this fruit is
nauseous, disagreeable, and worthless: that represents the
Lutheran Church. And now I will show you the holy Ap-
ostolic Church." Suiting his action to his words, he cracked
the nut, and, lo and behold! to his utter chagrin and discom-
fiture the inside contents were perfectly decayed and rotten.

(3.) Study the analogies between the object shown and the
truth to be taught. In 1 Kings xxii, 11, 34, 35, we have the
case of an object-lesson that sounded very well, but the
analogy failed to hold good. A preacher, using hot and cold
air as an illustration, said, "The more you heat the air in a
receiver the more room there is to put in more air." Another preacher announced as his text, "Thou makest my feet
like hen's feet," and used the analogy of their clinging to
the roost to teach the duty of clinging to the cross. Such
mistakes may usually be avoided by preparing the lesson
before attempting to teach it.

TEACHING: (1.) By means of careful questions get the
scholars to mention the qualities of the object as far as they
are to be used. A teacher should expect peculiar answers
at times, and take them good-naturedly, without being discon-

certed. A reverend gentleman was addressing a school recently, and was trying to enforce the idea that the hearts of the little ones were sinful and needed regulating. Taking his watch and holding it up, he said : "Now, here is my watch ; suppose it don't keep good time—now goes too fast, and now too slow—what shall I do with it ?" "Sell it !" shouted a flaxen-headed youngster.

(2.) Call the attention of the class to the Scripture passages, and have a part of them, at least, memorized.

(3.) By questions and explanations make the analogies between the object and the truth clear, and then remove the object from sight.

Hartley, in his "Pictorial Teaching," gives an amusing example of confounding truth with an illustration. A teacher was one day explaining to a class of girls the nature of faith, and by way of illustration pointed through the window to a boat which could be seen upon the river. "Look," said the teacher, "at that boat. You can see it, can you not ?" "Yes," said the scholars. "Well, if I were to tell you that there was a mutton pie in the boat under the seat, would you believe me ?" "Certainly we should," they replied. "Well," said the teacher, "that is faith." A short time afterward the teacher was again talking to the children on a similar subject, and, asking the question, "What is faith ?" was astonished to hear the reply, "*Faith, teacher, is a mutton pie in a boat.*"

(4.) Impress the truth deeply upon the heart, and always close with personal application and prayer. One should always be careful that the truth shall reach the scholar's thoughts more deeply than the object, the latter ever keeping its place as a forerunner simply, and crying, "The truth that cometh after me is greater than I." *

* For specimen object-lessons embodying these principles, see those of Miss Timanus in the Appendix.

4

Seed - Thought for Object - Lessons.

The Fan and Sieve. Luke iii, 17 ; xxii, 31.

The sieve is used, of course, to sift out the good flour, and leave only the useless bran, and so the devil desires to sift out all that is good in us and leave only what is bad.   The fan, in Eastern countries, on the other hand, is used to fan away the chaff, and leave only pure wheat, (see Bible Dictionary,) and so Christ would purge us of "the chaff" of our natures and leave only "the wheat of our highest virtue."   Satan can only "*desire*" to sift us ; Christ can only "*pray* for us " that we may come to his purging—the decision is our own.

Having a fan and sieve, with these seed-thoughts an interesting object-lesson may be given.   See also Psa. i, 4 ; Isa. i, 25.

The Watch

has been used in various ways for object-lessons.   There are three excellent lessons that may be taught with it: 1. The world shows evidence of a Creator and Preserver.   Show the intricate machinery and the wonderful workings of the watch.   These could not become so by chance or accident.   Some one made them with a purpose.   Find by questions that the watch would cease to tick if it were not wound up and cared for, and teach the lesson of God's preserving care. 2. The heart must be right if we would have the life right.   Show that it is of no use to fix the hands simply ; the main-spring must be right, and then the hands will keep right.   So in us the relation of heart and hand. 3. We are immortal.   This truth has been taught to very small children by a watch taken out of its case, and the children led to notice that the watch still ticks, although out of its case.   Then, the case being put out of sight in one hat and the watch in another, they are led to notice that they can still hear the ticking, although it is unseen as well as separate from its cause.   So the body is only the case of the soul which can live after the separation by death.

A Photograph

may be used in this way : After general questions, bring out the fact that it is made by the sunshine in the dark camera, with somebody before it. Afterward show that from the darkness of repentance, when the Holy Ghost shines upon our hearts and Christ stands before them, they come forth in the likeness of Christ.

Miss M. I. Hanson, Instructor in Object Teaching in the Massachusetts State Normal School at Salem, also the teacher of an infant class, has contributed the following religious object-lessons for this work:

1. PURE HEARTS.

I take for my objects three paper hearts, one perfectly white, another with blots of ink on it, a third nearly covered with ink. I get from the children the statements that one heart is white, or pure, the others have blots of ink on them; then speak of their own hearts: are they like the pure white one, or have they blots on them? Get the statement that their hearts have blots of sin on them; mention different sins (little wrong words, deeds, thoughts, and looks) which make these blots on the heart; then also that the more wicked the heart the blacker. Then, going back to paper hearts, ask how to get the ink blots off. Children say, "By washing;" then, speaking of their sin-blotted hearts, ask what will cleanse them; will water? Get the statement, "Blood of Jesus Christ." Then have written upon the blackboard these sentences: "We have blots of sin on our hearts;" "The blood of Jesus Christ, his Son, cleanseth us from all sin."

Now the heart is cleansed by the blood of Christ, does it seem like the pure white heart? What does the Bible say of those that have pure hearts? Write on the blackboard, "Blessed are the pure in heart, for," etc. Speak of appearing before God on the last day with a sin-blotted heart, and, without daring to *see* him, *hearing* him say, "Depart," etc. Then speak of appearing before him with a heart cleansed by Jesus' blood, and *looking* upon him with joy unutterable as he says, "Come, ye blessed," etc. Then ask if any want their hearts cleansed; if they know where to go for this wonderful blood that can take away sin. No man can give it. Children answer, "Pray for it." Ask if any would like to ask Christ *now* for his cleansing blood, then close with a prayer for pure hearts.

2. CLEAN HANDS.

"Who shall ascend into the hill of the Lord?" "He that hath clean hands and a pure heart."

I take for my object the hands of the children—tell them to stand and hold up their hands—get from them various uses of hands; also draw from them the term "clean," as usually applied; then show that God calls those hands clean which are put to a good use. Have children mention numerous good things which their hands can do, and write them on the blackboard; then show that hands which look very clean to us may be very unclean in God's sight, because he knows whether they have been doing right or not. Then ask what God says of those who have clean hands. Have the verse repeated, and write it on the blackboard.

THE TONGUE.—Text: James iii, 8; Mark x, 27.

Lead the children to say we use our tongues to speak both good and wicked, kind and unkind words. To give an idea of control, refer to the wild caprices of a colt, how impossible it is to use him until he has been tamed. Tell the story of a boy whose tongue was always running into wicked speeches. It needed to be *tamed*. A colt cannot be tamed without a bridle, a tongue cannot be tamed without Christ's help.

Who of you have promised yourselves not to say wrong words ever again? Did you keep your promise? No. Why not? Our tongues·said the word before we knew it. So it seems that you need some one to watch and tame your tongues for you; you do not seem able to do it yourselves. The Bible says you cannot do it yourselves. Let me read: (James iii, 8.) Who will help you? Can you do it then? Let me read again from the Bible: (Mark x, 27.) Print the latter text upon the blackboard, and require the children to read.

THE WITHERED LEAF.

Rev. Alfred Cookman preached his last sermon, with a withered leaf in his hand as an object-lesson, on the text, "We all do fade as a leaf." By collecting, with the Concordance, all the passages in the Bible on the leaf, and ascertaining its natural history and attributes, many very excellent lessons may be drawn from it.

THE MAGNET LESSON.

Rev. E. P. Hammond gives a very effective lesson with the magnet, trying it first with an old spike, and finding it unable to draw it—illustrating the difficulty of moving those who have lived long in sin to love Christ. He then puts the magnet among a lot of tacks, which quickly fasten upon it, illustrating the readiness with which the children come to Jesus, and not only that, but also draw others by the love of Christ within them. Putting the magnet here again among the tacks, he shows how those tacks which adhere draw others and hold them. Many beautiful lessons may be drawn from the magnet by experiment and study.

THE VINE.   John xv, 1–10.

This has been effectively used by G. E. A. Moore, of St. Louis, and others. A knife, opened, is extended to the vine to cut it. "Shall I cut it?" "No." "Why?" "It would kill it." "Would it bear fruit if cut off?" "No." "No more shall *we* except we abide in Christ."

The taking away of the nipped grapes that others may be larger, the kindness of purging, the destruction of the useless, the sap that gives the branches life as Christ gives us life, these and many other points may be brought out by the teacher, after studying the vine, the passage referred to and others regarding the " empty vine," " wild grapes," etc., and then questioning the scholars.

The Lily.

Take a large white lily in full bloom, and read, as you hold it before the school, Matt. vi, 28–33. Then ask the school to " consider," (that is, ponder over and over again, as the original signifies,) to " consider the lilies," and learn three lessons: 1. A lesson to doubt and skepticism—" Consider the lilies *how* they grow," how *mysteriously* they grow. Thus critical skepticism, that will not believe any thing it cannot understand, is rebuked. Show how " curiously and wonderfully made " are the lilies. 2. A lesson to human pride—" Solomon in all his glory was not arrayed like one of these." Central Park is not as grand as Yosemite. The best wax bouquet is not equal to a garden. 3. A lesson to " little faith "—" Consider the lilies *how prosperously they grow* without toil or spinning, and shall not God much more care for us? " Find in the Concordance other references to the lily, and also ascertain peculiarities of Eastern lily from Bible Dictionary.

"A father giveth good gifts to his children." "God clothes the lily of the field." - - -

HOW MUCH MORE WILL GOD CLOTHE**ARE FOR US!**

.Although we have not yet spoken about the blackboard, we insert the above as a companion exercise for the object-lesson on the lily. Generally the blackboard and objects should be used together.

The Tares. A Bunch of Wheat with a Bunch of Weeds. Matt. xiii, 24–30. Text, Matt. xiii, 30.

Point: Now is the day of grace—afterward will be the time of reckoning.
I. Comparison between wheat and tares. Let the teacher show some stalks of wheat and some worthless weeds, each with the roots. Children point to each kind, and give the name. Which has done some good work? What will the wheat do for people? Give them life and strength. What good have the weeds done? Sometimes weeds make poison, which gives people much trouble. Do the wheat and the tares grow in the same or in

different fields? The tares grow among the wheat. Upon which does God's sun shine the brightest? etc., etc. The whole subject may be developed in this line by the teacher or superintendent.

THE DEW-DROPS AND RAIN-DROPS.

Take a bunch of flowers into the school with dew or rain drops upon them. Then tell these two stories: A little rain-drop the other day, before the rain, was looking down from the sky, and its little heart felt sad to see how withered and dry all the flowers and the grass seemed to be. Then it said, "Though I am only a little drop, I will go down and kiss that weary and dusty blade of grass." So it came, and the grass looked up and smiled. Another drop, when it saw how much its brother had done, said, "Well, I'll go, too, and kiss that fading violet." It came, and the violet rejoiced. Then the other drops said, "Let us go too." And down they came, one after another, until there was a shower that made all the gardens laugh for joy. So our little words and deeds may make others happy.

The following was given by Rev. E. L. Hyde, at a Band of Hope meeting, on the same object: "Children, what did you see on the grass this morning that sparkled so?" "Dew." Then get the children to tell what makes clouds, snow-flakes, etc. Call the snow "*The dew-drop's cousin,*" or, as a little child called it, "Rain all popped out white." Then, "What makes the engine go?" "Steam." "What besides fire does it take to make steam?" "Water." "Yes, and the water is made of a great many little drops. Each of them is a little fairy giant, and they say to each other, 'Let's make it go,' and then they bend all their little shoulders against the sides of the boiler, and push, and you hear the sound, 's-s-s-sh,' and the wheels begin to roll, and away it goes. So each of you has power to do something in pushing for the right. The smallest can 'push a pound.'"

POWER OF PRAYER.

A revolutionary sword may be used as an object-lesson. We keep it only as a curiosity to remember what it did "in our fathers' days, in the times of old," but not as the sword of the Spirit; (this may be drawn on the board.) It should not hang up as a relic, reminding us of three thousand slain in one day at Pentecost, but unused at present. It still has the pentecostal temper in its blade. Or use some Continental currency as a contrast to God's promises, which are never at a discount, never out of date, never curiosities of a departed government, but always "Yea and Amen in Christ Jesus."

RENEWED IN CHRIST.

Taking a bunch of old rags, and also some fine writing paper, use them with the following story from *The Sunday-School Times,* by **Dr. Todd:**

The Queen was riding out in her grand carriage, the horses tossing their plumes as if they felt themselves a little better than common horses, and the footmen all decked out in red, feeling that they had something royal about them. The Queen had always had every thing she wanted, and so was quite miserable because she could not think of a want to supply, or a new place to visit.

At last she bethought her that they had just been building a new paper-mill a few miles out of the city. Now she had never seen a paper-mill, and so she determined to stop a little way off, there leave her carriage, and walk in, not as a queen, but as an unknown, common lady. She went in alone, and told the owner she would like to see his mill. He was in a great hurry, and did not know that she was the Queen. But he said to himself, "I can gratify the curiosity of this lady, and add to her knowledge; and though I am terribly hurried, yet I will do this kindness." He then showed her all the machinery, how they bleach the rags and make them white; how they grind them into pulp; how they make sheets, and smooth them, and dry them, and make them beautiful. The Queen was astonished and delighted. She would now have something new to think about and talk about.

Just as she was about leaving the mill she came to a room filled with old worn-out, dirty rags. At the door of this room was a great multitude of poor, dirty men and women and children bringing old bags on their backs filled with bits of rags and paper, parts of old newspapers, and the like, all exceedingly filthy. These were rag-pickers, who had picked these old things out of the streets and gutters of the great city.

"What do you do with all these vile things?" said the Queen.

"Why, madam, I make paper out of them. To be sure, they are not very profitable stock, but I can use them, and it keeps these poor creatures in bread."

"But these rags! Why, sir, they are of all colors, and how do you make them white?"

"O, I have the power of taking out all the dirt and the old colors. You see that 'scarlet' and that 'crimson,' yet I can make even scarlet and crimson, the hardest colors, to remove and become white as snow."

"Wonderful, wonderful!" said the Queen.

She then took her leave, but the polite owner of the mill insisted on walking and seeing her safe in her carriage. When she got in and bowed to him with a smile, and he saw all the grand establishment. he knew it was the Queen.

"Well, well!" said he, "she has learned something at any rate. I wish it may be a lesson in true religion."

A few days after the Queen found lying upon her writing-desk a pile of the most beautiful polished paper she had ever seen. On each sheet were

the letters of her own name and her own likeness. How she did admire it!
She found, also, a note within, which she read. It ran thus:

"Will my Queen be pleased to accept a specimen of my paper, with the
assurance that every sheet was manufactured out of the contents of those
dirty bags which she saw on the backs of the poor rag-pickers? All the
filth and the colors are washed out, and I trust the result is such as even a
queen may admire. Will the Queen also allow me to say, that I have had
many a good sermon preached to me in my mill? I can understand how
our Lord Jesus Christ can take the poor heathen, the low, sinful creatures
every-where, viler than the rags, and wash them and make them clean; and
how, 'though their sins be as scarlet, he can make them whiter than snow;
and though they be red like crimson, he can make them as wool.' And I
can see that he can write his own name on their foreheads, as the Queen will
find *her* name on each sheet of paper; and I can see how, as these filthy
rags may go into the palace and be ever admired, some poor, vile sinners
may be washed in the blood of the Lamb, and be received into the palace
of the great King in heaven.   THE MILL OWNER."

LIVING WATER.*

The following may furnish suggestions to be used with a fountain or a
glass of water if the circumstances mentioned cannot be realized:

"Whosoever drinketh of this water" said Jesus, "shall thirst again; but
whosoever drinketh of the water that I shall give him shall *never thirst;* but
the water that I shall give shall be in him a well of water springing up into
everlasting life."

Here Christ represents the gift of the Spirit as "living water," which
satisfies our longings as nothing else can do. While at every well of earthly
pleasure we must day after day draw again and again for a temporary grati-
fication of our thirst for happiness, he who takes into his heart this "fountain of the indwelling Spirit" shall "*never thirst*" for other draughts, but
"with joy shall he draw water out of the wells of salvation." And "*every
one* that thirsteth may come to these waters" and be satisfied. "Ye weary
and heavy laden" with long years of constant effort to draw up happiness
from other wells, say to the Master to-day, "Give me of this water, that I
thirst not, neither *come hither to draw."* And not only will the Spirit of God
save us from the feverish "*thirst*" of *human life,* but he will also be in us "a
well of water *springing up into everlasting life."*

Yesterday I went for meditation to our beautiful Lindenwood Cemetery.
After passing the gate I stopped a moment to look at the Soldiers' Monument,
man's fitting tribute to the brave. But a few steps further on I paused in still
greater admiration before a *new* monument—*God's monument to the Christian.*

* See Frontispiece.

Man's chisel never wrought so beautifully! Human hands never arranged such diamonds and pearls in so stately a pillar of silver!

The monument bore no name and no epitaph, but it stood in its matchless beauty amid the tombstones and monuments as God's tribute to those whose "names are written in heaven." Many of you have seen it—the monument of ice through which the fountain unceasingly sends its water into the air. All through the winter the fountain has defied the cold and sparkled daily in the sun. Glorious picture of the true Christian! What though the snows and frost of the world's coldness gather about him, there is "in him a well of water springing up into everlasting life" that cannot be frozen, and his joy and singing leap above all temptation and "rejoice evermore." What though death with his chilly hand touch his body and make it icy with death, there is "in him a well of water springing up into *everlasting life*," and, like the fountain, rising triumphantly above the ice around it, the "living water" of our hearts rises to the better life: the fountain must rise as high as its source. Rude and playful boys stained the icy monument with the mud of their feet and marred it with their axes, but still the sparkling stream threw its jewels into the sunlight. Men may persecute and revile the Christian and speak all manner of evil against him, but above it all leaps the "living water" of his inward joy and shouts "*Blessed.*"

The aperture through which the water rose I saw filled up with a block of ice, and for a little time the stream was repressed; but very soon it cut its way out, and rose with its triumphant joy into the air again.

The grave may endeavor to bind down the Christian's spirit with its clods; the "living water that springs up into everlasting life" shall break through them and cry, "O grave, where is thy victory?"

In this monument of ice and snow I saw God's sculpturing of the prayer, "Wash me, and I shall be whiter than snow;" God's chiseling of the promise, "Though your sins be as scarlet, they shall be white as snow."

And then, as I thought of the "everlasting life" and the "glorified bodies" of the saints in light, I saw the monument transfigured to a heavenly meaning, and heard a voice, the voice of my hope, saying, "Who are these in *white robes*, and whence came they?" And then I saw in it another picture of the overcomer made "a pillar in the temple of his God."

If I should wish for any monument to rise in memory of my life besides that best of all monuments, "The good we have done," I should ask that in the purest marble such an ice monument should be represented, and, through it, and above it, should play an unfailing fountain, and on the marble should be cut: "*The water that I shall give him shall be in him a well of water springing up into everlasting life.*"

V. MAP TEACHING.

Little need be said in regard to the use of maps, as they have been long and widely used in the Sunday-school.

It would be an improvement, perhaps, to the present method of hanging maps, if they were all hung at the most central point for the eyes of the whole school, only one being unrolled at a time, that one, of course, being the one which gives the geography of the lesson. Besides this, every teacher should have a portable Atlas * for his own class. Besides their use for ordinary geographical reference, maps may be used for Bible lectures and reviews. In the latter case, by pointing to the waters, mountains, and towns associated with the last three, or six, or twelve months' study, and asking questions as to the events associated with these geographical points, and giving such explanations as may be required, the facts learned will be strongly impressed on the mind with the help of the eye.

We give the following suggestions for a catechetical and descriptive Bible lecture, with the map of Palestine. Subject: "From Dan to Beersheba." Show the position of "Dan and Beersheba," and also that the expression means the same in regard to Palestine as "from the Atlantic to the Pacific" in regard to the United States. Divide the school, two Sabbaths before the lecture, into three traveling parties, one of them to go from BEERSHEBA to the Mediterranean coast, and then up the coast to Sidon, and across to Dan, studying all incidents of Bible history associated with any of the places through which they would pass, as Gaza, (Samson, Philip,) Joppa, (Peter,) Cæsarea, (Peter, Paul, etc.,) Mount Carmel, (Elijah, Elisha,) Tyre, (Solomon,) Sarepta, (Jesus,) Sidon, Mount Hermon, Damascus, (Paul,) DAN.

* The little pamphlet Atlas published by Nelson & Phillips is one of the very best in quality and variety, and yet is sold at a very low price. These same maps are bound into Whitney's Bible Geography, which should be in every teacher's library as a help to map teaching.

The second party to go from BEERSHEBA across to the Dead Sea, (notice Zoar, Sodom and Gomorrah, Edom, Moab, and Mount Pisgah overlooking the whole;) then up the Jordan (notice its crossing by the Israelites, its waters parted by the prophet's mantle; Jericho, a little way from its banks, whose walls fell, waters were healed, etc., the brook Jabbok that flows into it, Jacob's wrestling-place) to the Sea of Galilee, and coast along its western shore, stopping at Gadara, (demoniac;) then up to the continuation of the Jordan, through to the waters of Merom to Cæsarea Philippi, (Jesus,) and across to DAN.

The third party to go through the center of the country from BEERSHEBA to Hebron, (Abraham,) to Bethlehem, (David, Ruth, Jesus,) to Jerusalem, (see Bible Dictionary, etc.,) to Mount of Olives, (Gethsemane, Ascension, David's retreat, etc.,) to Bethany, (Lazarus, spikenard, etc.,) to Bethel, (Jacob, etc.,) to Gilgal, (Joshua,) to Shechem, (Jacob's well,) stopping to climb Mount Gerizim, (Samaritan temple, blessings and curses,) and Mount Ebal to Samaria, (God's deliverance, etc.;) to Dothan, (Joseph,) to Mount Gilboa, (Saul, etc.,) to Nain, (Jesus,) to Nazareth, (Jesus,) to Cana, (wine,) to Mount Tabor and Mount of Beatitudes; then to the lower part of the Sea of Galilee, and up the eastern coast to Tiberias, (miracles,) Bethsaida, (miracles,) Chorazin, (curses;) then across the sea, recalling the voyages of Christ and his apostles, (the two storms, two draughts of fishes, etc.;) then across the country to DAN.

Teachers and scholars having studied their Bibles and Bible Dictionaries, with their maps, and being prepared to make these three trips, with a knowledge of all the historical associations, the lecturer, with pictures, relics from the East, and incidents from books of travel, can make these journeys very interesting and instructive. A similar lecture can be made with the map of the Israelites' Journey, called "From Rameses to Jerusalem;" and another on the map of the Journeys of St. Paul, called "From Damascus to Rome."

VI. PICTURE TEACHING.

When our parlors are full of Bible pictures, and scarcely a scene in the Bible has not been represented by some master hand, it is strange that Bible pictures have not been used more extensively in Sunday-school teaching. If a school can afford it, the colored pictures on stiff card-board, that are published by our Sunday-School Unions, should be in its " *Cabinet for Eye-Teaching ;*" but if there are not means to secure these, a great many pictures may be borrowed from the homes of those in the Church who have well-furnished walls. An infant-class teacher can make even a familiar picture very useful in securing attention. If the lesson be about " Christ in the Manger," one of the many pictures of that scene will afford the best means of making the lesson clear. In almost every community pictures may be found of the leading events of Bible history.*

Besides this, every teacher should have his own Picture Scrap-Book. The illustrated papers will frequently give a picture that may be used some time to illustrate Bible truth. One teacher writes thus to the " Sunday-School Journal :"

" I have a scrap-book in which I am collecting pictures illustrative of the Bible. I buy up every engraving of every sort by which any fact or custom of the Bible may be illus-

---

* In the Bible House at New York a room has been fitted up, called the Sunday-School Exchange, in which may be found a reference library of all the best works published on the Sunday-school cause, which teachers are free to come and consult. All Sunday-school periodicals are also kept on file ; also a stock of pictures, maps, and objects suitable for illustrating the Bible have been collected, any of which the teacher may have the privilege of renting.

One of the very best, and by far the cheapest, of helps for picture teaching is the " Bible Roll," by Samuel W. Clark. (Published by Nelson & Phillips.) It comprises twenty-five large views of the tabernacle, temple, Eastern manners, customs, etc. The costumes of the priests, the altars, tables, vails, and other parts of the great symbolic tabernacle, are clearly represented. A school cannot spend five dollars in pictures to better advantage than in securing this valuable collection.

trated. I find Nelson's cards of great value. Already my scrap-book is an attraction to old and young. I hold an occasional 'tea-table talk' with my Sunday scholars as my guests, and the scrap-book makes the time fly. Several times I have taken it with me for use in my class. No trouble to 'get the attention' of my scholars."

VII. THE BLACKBOARD.

The blackboard excels the six other forms of eye teaching in convenience, availability, and cheapness. Description and stories require more time to reach the heart through the ear than the blackboard to reach it through the eye. Objects are shown but once, while the blackboard may be used again and again for an indefinite time. Pictures have one unchanging surface, while the blackboard gives opportunity for fresh and varied illustrations. Maps are purchased at considerable expense, and a school cannot usually supply itself with a sufficient number for thorough study of Bible Geography. Blackboard maps may present the towns, rivers, and mountains mentioned in the lesson and their vicinity more prominently than any published maps would do it.

The general advantages of the Sunday-school blackboard are,

1. To save time. Certain hymns of which there may be but few copies can be slowly taught to the school by repetition; write the words on the blackboard, and they are known *at once.* A contrast is to be expressed between good and evil, or between joy and sorrow. Half an hour would do it in spoken words; put them in opposite colors or positions on the blackboard and the contrast is at once apparent. A wrong idea is to be presented and overthrown. How much a long argument may be condensed by writing the wrong idea upon the blackboard, and then destroying it with the eraser to make room for writing the truth, or by canceling it with the truth written over it!

2. To give variety, vividness, and clearness. A new motto, a new analysis, a new outline, greets us every Sabbath. The ear having been taught during the study of the lesson, at its close the eye is given the same truth and the "dead bones live." A few bold letters or a distinct outline applied to the lesson at the close of its study, and it stands forth in stereoscopic clearness to the mind.

3. To concentrate attention and thought. Rev. Dr. Vincent once illustrated the power of the chalk and blackboard to win attention by taking a crayon in his hand at a Sunday-school Institute and raising it toward the blackboard. The whole audience eagerly followed his hand, but he dropped it to his side, saying, "I am not going to write any thing; I only wanted to show how quickly I could concentrate your attention by raising the chalk."

THE SLATE.

To the individual teacher the slate is as helpful as the blackboard to the pastor or superintendent. All that may be said of the advantages of the latter to the school may be said of the former in regard to the class. Every teacher who can write a plain hand, even though unskillful with the pencil, may use the slate with great profit.

Nearly every exercise in this book may be used with a slate by each teacher in his class as appropriately as on the black-board for the whole school.

Every scholar also should have a slate to bring a map of the scene of the lesson, written answers of questions given out the previous Sabbath by the superintendent or teacher, written epitomes of the home readings or of the stories, in the lesson, a copy of the black-board exercise of the preceding Sabbath, or the analysis of the lesson for the day.

The slate may be made as useful in Sunday-school as in day-school. The simplest outlines and a half dozen words written upon a slate by the teacher will fix the points of the lesson in the mind more quickly and vividly than any words, as shown by the foregoing illustration of the story of Zaccheus.

ABUSES.

Some things are too sacred for chalk or pencil; an out line of Christ in the form of a man is one of these. Put away your chalk as you approach such "holy ground." Nor are such exercises to be commended as are chiefly re-markable for the skill of the artist, and lead us to say, "How fine!" instead of "How true!" Generally the simplest outlines should be the highest attempts of blackboard delineation, and simple word exercises should be used far more frequently than outlines.

One * who is well known in the Sunday-school work writes these well-timed words on the abuse of the blackboard: "I am fully conscious, as all who have thoughtfully observed the course of this line of teaching, I think, must be, that it has been made the victim of most absurd exaggerations and complicated follies. Intended to be the simplest, the clear-est, and the most vivid of methods, it has been made by a large class of blackboard delineators a vehicle of the most extravagant imaginations and the most absurdly unimpress-ive exercises. What I have always pleaded for in its use, and do now more than ever, is pith, point, clearness, concise-ness, the latter especially. Sensations are not the want of the hour. Common sense is the staple now as it ever has been."

Rev. J. S. Ostrander gives similar cautions against abuses as follows ·

1. It must not be made a hobby. It has its important and

* James H. Kellogg.

proper work, but may be abused. It is not every thing, any more than the organ, the maps, or the singing of the school. Here, then, first of all, we enter our *protest* against the blackboard hobbyist.

2. Do not attempt lengthy written exercises. Short texts, brief statements, concise analyses, will be more useful, as a general rule, than blackboards covered with writing which "darkeneth counsel by words."

3. Never employ an aimless illustration. Never say of a pleasant conceit or diagram, "This would make a good blackboard exercise," for if it do not fix more deeply in the mind a truth, then it is useless and aimless.

4. Extravagant elaboration should be avoided in picture or object illustration. Simplicity in drawing finds no critics; but to attempt perfection with chalk is a waste of time, and above the appreciation of the mass of children.

5. Reject all personification, etc., which may so easily become mere comicalities. They are evil continually. Some have attempted to represent Satan, hell, the judgment, etc. This lowers the standard of truth, produces levity, and defeats the object sought. No pencil or chalk sketch within the capacity of a blackboard can convey such an idea of those terrible facts as will justify the doubtful undertaking.

6. Blackboard "exhibitions" should never appear when addressing children. Avoid all display; seek ease in the use of crayons. The presence of the first, and the want of the latter, has spoiled many a good point, which was lost in the "exhibition of the blackboard."

The following contribution on "Simple Blackboarding," by Rev. J. F. Clymer, of Pittsfield, Mass., will be found eminently practical and suggestive:

SIMPLE BLACKBOARDING.

The blackboard, like many good people, is much abused. It is denounced for Sunday-school work, because some have used it to exhibit artistic skill in the *use* of God's truth, thus making truth the servant of art. Truth and art should serve each other; but in the king's palace art must be the servant of his law. When God's law is made the *servant* of art in Sunday-school blackboarding, no wonder honest natures are disgusted.

The primary object of the blackboard in Sunday-school is to illustrate God's truth. When this is not done the most skillful chalking is unproductive of good. The use of the blackboard for illustrating Bible truths is condemned by some of our best thinkers for its materialistic tendencies. It is urged that the use of material objects for presenting truth leads the mind into the errors of materialism. God did not think so while teaching the Jews the principles of Judaism. He thundered on Sinai that they might HEAR him in his power and wrath; but this was not enough; they had eyes as well as ears, and he *wrote* his law on leaves of stone that they might SEE him in its truths, and then commanded them to "*write* these words on the posts of their houses, and on their gates." When Belshazzar was to be condemned, God had no fear of materializing that besotted king by writing his death-warrant on the wall of his palace.

Jesus was willing to trust the materialistic tendencies of his sermon written on the ground, that voiceless sermon which sent the captious Jews away in self-condemning silence. When Jesus wrote this sermon on the ground he "stooped down." A little spiritual stooping would help our blackboarding amazingly. Unwillingness to do the plain, simple, materialistic thing on the blackboard keeps many a superintendent from making it a power for the truth of God in his school. If our ideas of blackboarding had a little more *heart* and a little less *art* about them, the plainest sort of a man for superintendent would find that chalk and blackened boards would help him wonderfully to honor Jesus. In behalf of the modest, the unartistic, and the unskillful, I earnestly plead for simple blackboarding.

At the opening of school any superintendent may secure order by placing the number of the hymn on the blackboard. The silent figuring will notify every one in the room of the number of the hymn to be sung; it will also secure attention and silence, and will save much bell-ringing and talk. And more than this, those that come in during the singing may find the hymn without disturbing others, and join in the opening services immediately.

The Golden Text, accompanying the Berean Series of Bible Lessons, may be put on the blackboard with the rudest sort of lettering. This will catch wandering eyes during the hour of recitation, and possibly bring wandering thoughts back to the lesson again.

Sometimes a single word will be a key to the whole lesson. In the Berean Series, in the lesson entitled "Help One Another," Rom. xv, 1-7, the simple word HELP put upon the blackboard in large plain letters will be full of significant suggestions to all, such as "*Our* need of *Help*," "*Help* comes from God," "We must *Help* each other," etc.

An easy topical development of the lesson may be made at the review and put upon the blackboard in another form. In the lesson on "Naaman and the little Slave Girl," 2 Kings v, 1-7, the question may be put to the school, "Whom is our lesson about to-day, a man, woman, boy, or girl?" Yes; a girl.

Put the word "girl" and what is said of her on the blackboard thus, being sure to develop the facts from the school:

$$\text{GIRL} \left\{ \begin{array}{l} \text{LITTLE} \\ \text{SLAVE} \\ \text{POOR} \\ \text{GOOD} \end{array} \right. \quad \textbf{DID} \quad \begin{array}{l} \text{What she could.} \\ \\ \text{Good for evil.} \end{array}$$

These facts, with but little thought and less skill, can be easily drawn from any school that may have merely read this lesson, and then the application of the two practical lessons educed, namely, "We must do our duty *always*," and "Overcome evil with good."

From the lesson on "Our Reasonable Service," Rom. xii, 1–18, draw from the school, by suitable questions, the idea that "All we have is from God," and then show how reasonable it is that all we have should be used for God; and while you talk these thoughts to the ear with your voice, make the blackboard talk them to the eye, thus:

ALL ^{FROM}_{FOR} GOD.

WHY?   "Ye are bought with a price."

In the lesson on the "Lamb in the midst of the throne," Rev. vii, 9–17, St. John in his vision sees the multitude in heaven who came out of great tribulation. Where had they tribulation? On earth. HERE. Where did he see them? In heaven. THERE. Have the words "Here" and "There" on the blackboard, with the facts of the lesson, in the following manner:

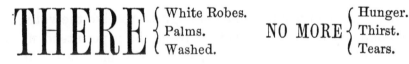

| THERE | { White Robes. Palms. Washed. | NO MORE | { Hunger. Thirst. Tears. |

| HERE | { Great Tribulation. Hunger. Thirst. Tears. |

The locality of the words "Here" and "There" will suggest the idea of heaven and earth silently, but forcibly.

The calling the names of teachers, and sometimes of the scholars, to get the number present, etc., consumes a great deal of precious time to very little effect. Let the secretary get the number of teachers and scholars present by counting them from his position at his desk, and then just at the close of recitation, or immediately before the review, he may put his report on the blackboard in this way, or in any other way that may be suggestive:

No. of Teachers		40
" "	present	35
	absent	5

How shall we supply their places?

No. of Scholars		300
" "	present	230
"	absent	70

Where are they?

This will occupy the time of no one but the secretary, and that for only a few minutes, and then the whole school at a glance can get a knowledge of the situation, and possibly be prompted to have the figures on the board tell a better story on the following Sabbath.

Any man who has influence enough to receive the votes of any company of men and women to be the superintendent of their Sabbath-school has *ability* to use the blackboard if he only has *willingness* to use it in this simple, unostentatious way.

The plainest sort of a man, with the lesson in his head and heart, baptized with the spirit of self-forgetfulness, whose only aim is to impress God's truth on youthful hearts, will do more with his rudest chalkings than the skillful blackboardist with perfect diagrams, but without his Christly spirit and aim.

MATERIALS WANTED.

A large revolving blackboard is of course the best. It affords a great advantage in that the exercise on one surface may front the school during the lesson and another exercise may be held in reserve on the hidden side for the closing review. Often it is well to have a simple exercise on the front, such as a motto or a word exercise; a symbol exercise or outline exercise being kept on the reverse side until the other has been used. Some carpenter interested in the school will sometimes make such a blackboard at a low price, but its great usefulness will be an ample reward for an extra effort to obtain it. Those who are building new churches should put in a fine wall blackboard. If neither of these can be had, a poor one is far better than none. Then a good eraser, a long, stout rule, a good pointer, and a box of mixed crayons, will make an outfit. White crayons should generally be used, but other colors sometimes add greatly to the variety and strength of expression. By gaslight yellow crayons are most distinct. Use round chalk for writing, square chalk for printing. "Bear on! Speak loud to the eye!" A free and off-hand way of writing and printing should be cultivated.

The Scholars' Part in Blackboard Exercises.

The most excellent use of the blackboard is to draw from the scholars the information already imparted to them by their teachers. Uniform in most cases, the exercise should not be written or printed on the blackboard before the time when it is to be used, except perhaps a few catch-words and initials. Questions should then be asked, and the answers briefly indicated with the chalk, until the exercise is complete. Lines, dots, and letters will often be sufficient to hold the attention and impress the thought. Difficult exercises must generally be made before the school session; but all that can be drawn from the scholars by questions and readily delineated or printed should be left to the time of using the exercise. This will allow one to take advantage of childhood's curiosity, which loves to witness the creation of a thing.

In this book the exercises are usually given as they would appear when completed. As much as possible, the materials should be questioned out of the scholars. For example, let the board present at the opening of the exercise the following, previously printed upon it:

SIN

THE FATHER
THE SON LO AND GIVES
THE SINNER
THE SPIRIT

Then ask how the Father feels toward us, and what he gave us as his greatest gift. The same question in regard to the Son. Then ask, How were the Israelites saved from the bite of the serpent, to what are we to "look," and what do we give? Then, How does the Spirit feel toward us, and what does it give? The exercise at the close will be as follows:

SIN

The Father
The Son LO VES AND GIVES THE SON.
The Sinner OKS HIMSELF.
The Spirit VES HIMSELF.
SALVATION.

In an acrostic exercise, the acrostic letters may sometimes be put on beforehand; in a table exercise, the outline of the table; in a canceling or erasing exercise, that which is to be canceled or erased; in a map exercise, the simple outline without the points of importance indicated.

VARIETY AND EMPHASIS.

These are given by the colors, size, and position of the words. EMPHASIS.—1. The *size* of letters of course indicates degrees of importance. 2. *Position.* A word or two words having a whole line or standing alone are made prominent.

VARIETY.—1. Breaking up the sentences into long and short lines gives variety. 2. *Colors*, however, give opportunity for greater variety. References to Christ and his atonement should usually be in red; to nature, in green; to purity in

white; to precious things, in yellow. Sometimes two colors
may be used in the same letter as a double line of white and
red in Christ. (For use of colors see alphabet of symbols and
colors, page 185.) *Emphasis* may be illustrated by this exercise:

WHATSOEVER
THE LORD
HATH SAID UNTO
THEE
DO!

" Whatsoever," "thee," and " do," are made emphatic by
position; "the Lord," by *size* of letters. Variety may be illustrated by this exercise:

THE SHADOW
OF A
GREAT ROCK
IN A
Weary Land

The breaking up of the lines gives variety; and also putting
" Great Rock " in red as referring to Christ, and " Shadow "
in brown.

OUR DIVISIONS

Are suggested by our own experience, and the classes are
arranged in a natural order from the simplest to the most
difficult, from the simple motto to the more elaborate outline
exercise. Enough are given under each class to show distinctly what we mean by its name and to suggest many
others.

1. THE MOTTO EXERCISE.—The simplest form of black-

board exercise is to write or print the Golden Text, or a religious precept or proverb, or some motto or watchword, on the blackboard. By breaking it up into short lines, emphasizing important words by colors, large capitals, and a position by themselves, such mottoes are often made very impressive. The following is a good illustration of the arrangement of a motto on the blackboard:

"The Lord" "healeth" "thee" stand out prominent, both on account of position and size. "Healeth" should be in red, to suggest the cleansing blood, and "thee" in white, to represent "white as snow."

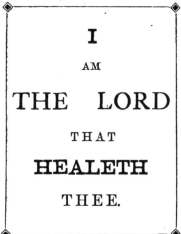

Even the writing of a simple precept on the blackboard about which you wish to speak impresses that precept on those who are listening as no emphasis or repetition can do.

MUCH WITH GOD, MUCH LIKE GOD.

Such a motto can be illustrated by the story of "that disciple whom Jesus loved," or by the story of Moses on the Mount, and enforced with such passages as, "We shall be like him, for we shall see him as he is," and, "We all, with open face beholding as in a glass the glory of the Lord, are changed into the same image." The following exercises are only suggestive of a multitude of others:

TRUST YE IN THE LORD FOREVER:

FOR IN THE

LORD JEHOVAH

IS EVERLASTING STRENGTH. Isa. xxvi, 4.

THE BLOOD OF
JESUS CHRIST HIS SON
CLEANSETH US
FROM ALL SIN.
1 JOHN i, 7.

(The first two lines in red, the last two in white.)

A story may often be nailed in the memory by placing its pivot sentence, its most important words, on the blackboard. For example, this motto and story:

"GOD IS NOWHERE."

An infidel was one day troubled in his mind as he sat in his room alone, while his little Nellie was away at Sunday-school. He had often said, "There is no God," but could not satisfy himself with his skepticism, and at this time he felt especially troubled as thoughts of the Sunday-school and of the wonderful works of creation would push their way into his mind. To quiet these troublesome thoughts he took some large cards and printed on each of them " *God is nowhere,*" and hung them up in his study. Nellie soon came home, and began to talk about God; but her father pointed her to one of the cards and said, "Can you read that?" She climbed a chair and began eagerly to spell it out: "G-o-d, God, i-s, is, n-o-w, now, h-e-r-e, here; God is now here. Is n't that right, papa? I know it is right—God is *now here.*" The man's heart was touched, and his infidelity banished, by the faith of Nellie, and again the prophecy was fulfilled, " A little child shall lead them."

Let the blackboard delineator then put a line under " now " to make it a separate word and also to emphasize it, and then teach the school from this motto and story that " God is not far from every one of us " in all that we do and say and think.

The Rev. Geo. A. Peltz recommends the use of the board as a bulletin, and for general sentiments as well as Scripture:

"Use it for special announcements. Much time is unnecessarily wasted in calling attention to the various matters connected with the economy of the school. The proper use of the blackboard here will greatly aid order and quiet. For example, how suggestive would be the display of a board neatly lettered, as follows:

NEXT SUNDAY

MISSIONARY COLLECTION

FOR

HEATHEN LANDS!

FREELY GIVE!   **FREELY GIVE!**

Or use the blackboard to express any general sentiment, or text, or motto, which may be appropriately made by any special event in your history. For example, on Easter Sunday let the board be conspicuously lettered, as follows:

'THE LORD IS RISEN.'

Or at Christmas let it be inscribed:

'JESUS IS BORN.'"

SEED-THOUGHT.

FOR THANKSGIVING DAY.—Print in the style indicated the following mottoes: "Eat the fat, and drink the sweet, and send portions unto them for whom nothing is prepared." "Not despising the riches of his goodness, and forbearance, and long-suffering."

LIFE OR DEATH.—The following motto, from one of the sermons of the Rev. T. De Witt Talmage, is good for the blackboard:

"Some theologians take four or five volumes in which to state their religious belief. I tell you all of my theology in one sentence: "Jesus Christ—take him and live; refuse him, and die."

SIN AND SORROW.—From the same source we give another motto exercise, when a single word may be used impressively.

"Ingenious little children sometimes tell you how, with a few letters, they can spell a very large word. With three letters I can spell *bereavement.* With three letters I can spell *disappointment.* With three letters I can spell *suffering.* With three letters I can spell *death.* With three letters I can spell *perdition.* S-i-n—SIN. That is the cause of all our trouble now. That is the cause of our trouble for the future."

"SIN" being printed very large, across it, in another color, may be written the words in italics; above it may then be written, "Christ will save us from ——," and on either side, "No —— in heaven."

II. THE TOPIC EXERCISE.

Next to the motto exercise in simplicity comes the topic exercise, which consists in putting the divisions of an address, or the analysis of a lesson, or the prominent points of a story, upon the blackboard, one after another. For example, "Christ's Miracles of Raising the Dead," by Rev. W. B. Wright:

  I. JAIRUS' DAUGHTER—from her BED.
  II. WIDOW'S SON—from his BIER.
  III. LAZARUS—from the TOMB.

This exercise illustrates the increasing wonder of the three miracles on the dead; one raised just after death from her "bed;" another a few hours after death from his "bier," as he was "carried forth;" and a third from the "tomb," where he had "lain four days already."

On this same subject the NATIONAL TEACHER gives some excellent suggestions by which this blackboard exercise may be expanded and illustrated:

1. The specially tender circumstances under which each of the three cases of raising the dead by Jesus was wrought, namely, an *only* daughter, twelve years old—an *only son* of a *widow*—an *only* brother of two orphaned, (?) self-dependent, (?) pious, loving sisters.

2. Jesus' way of sustaining faith when overstrained. Just when the crushing message comes, " Thy daughter is dead," he girds the ruler's faith with the divine assurance, " Be not afraid; only believe." What other incidents of like kind?

3. He who so often wept himself, so often says, "Weep not;" "Let not your heart be troubled;" "My peace I give unto you." The "Man of Sorrows," the Great Comforter.

4. Jesus' way of speaking of death. "The maid is not dead, but sleepeth;" "Lazarus sleepeth, and I go that I may wake him out of his sleep." The resurrection and the risen dead were such vivid realities to his omniscience that he could but deem death a mere sleep. So faith makes it to the Christian. . . . The awful sublimity, and yet the simple, self-assured style of his address to the dead: "Young man, I say unto thee, Arise;" "Lazarus, come forth·" "Maid, Arise." (The Syriac noun which Jesus used was a word of endearment, and signifies a lamb. It was as if he should say, "My dear lamb, arise.")

SEED-THOUGHT.

NOW AND HEREAFTER.—The following passage may be so broken up as to indicate its topics distinctly: "Now are we the sons of God; and it doth not yet appear what we shall be: but we know, 1. We shall be like him; 2. We shall see him as he is." ("Now" and "what we shall be" should each have a line and stand in contrast to each other; as also "it doth not yet appear" and "we know.")

THE CHRISTIAN'S LIBRARY.—This outline may be used for a talk on the wonderful harmony between nature, the Bible, Jesus, and Christian experience; Vol. I—"The Works of God;" Vol. II—"The Written Word;" Vol. III—"The Living Word;" Vol. IV—"The Living Epistles."

OUR COMMISSIONS.—The commissions to different ranks and classes may be written, one below the other, on the blackboard, or written on scrolls in imitation of parchment rolls.

Pulpit.—Preach the word. Pews—Let him that heareth

say, Come." Sunday-school Teachers—"Feed my lambs." Converts—"When thou art converted, strengthen thy brethren." Parents—"Take this child and nurse it for Me." Business men—" Not slothful in business, fervent in spirit." All—

WHATSOEVER GOD HATH SAID UNTO THEE, DO.
ye would that men should do to you, do ye even so to them,

THE SOWER.—SEED: 1. Stolen; 2. Scorched; 3. Choked; 4. Multiplied. (See Luke viii, 5-11.)

GOD'S BEST WORK.—The greatness of redemption above all the works of creation may be represented by this exercise: "God's best work." The heavens: "God's fingers." The waters: "Hollow of his hand." The isles: "He takes up as a very little thing." Salvation: (Isaiah:) "He made bare his arm;" (Mary:) "He showed strength with his arm."

It is the mystery of redemption that "the angels desire to look into"—redemption, that was the theme of Christ and of the saints from glory on the mount of transfiguration—redemption, that gives the singers of heaven their theme. In trouble God puts "under us his everlasting arms;" in darkness "still 'tis his hand that leadeth us;" if we sink into the waves, we only fall into the hollow of his hand; if we are deep in sin, the arm that was made bare reaches to the uttermost.

REVIVAL.—1. Time: "Now is the day of salvation." 2. Prayer: "Save now." 3. Duty: "Let him that heareth say, Come." 4. Result: "Added to the Church daily."

CHRIST'S BAPTISM.—Jesus—obeyed God—was baptized—prayed. 1. Heaven opened. 2. Dove descended. 3. Voice spake. Son standing: earth; Spirit descending: air; Father speaking: heaven.

LOVING AND SERVING.—John xxi, 13-19. The question—"Lovest thou me." The declaration—"Thou knowest that I love thee." The labor—"Feed my sheep; feed my lambs."

THE SUN OF RIGHTEOUSNESS.—By *Hattie N. Morris*, of New York.—She asked the question: "How many names is

Jesus called by?" Many were given by the audience. One of the answers, "the Sun of Righteousness," she had chosen for her lesson. What makes it so bright all around us? Put the outlines upon the blackboard: SUN GIVES LIGHT. A traveler may be lost at night in the woods, but coming day will reveal his path; so we were lost in sin until the Star of Bethlehem shone and the Sun of Righteousness arose on the earth. SUN GIVES HEAT. It warms the earth, unfolds leaf and blossom; so when our hearts are cold and lonely, Jesus' grace brings out blossoms of love and trust. SUN GIVES GROWTH. As plants grow in the warm beams, maturing flower and fruit, so the Sun of Righteousness draws out and strengthens every grace. Miss Morris then used a magnet and several needles, also a piece of steel. Thus Jesus draws to himself the little child as well as the older sinner. As the earth moves away the sun attracts it to itself again. So the SUN GIVES ATTRACTION. Thus Jesus says: "Turn ye, for why will ye die!" The longer the needles rest against the magnet, the harder is it to take them from it. So Jesus holds in strongest bonds the heart held nearest to himself. If we keep near this Sun of Righteousness he will give us Light, Heat, Growth, Attraction; for Jesus says: "And I, if I be lifted up from the earth, will draw all men unto me."

HARVEST.—The following words, written in lines one below the other, make a solemn lesson for the time of harvest: "The fruitless tree. Nothing but leaves. This year also. Cut it down." The encouraging view of the harvest of faithfulness may be represented with the following, broken up into seven or eight lines: "He that goeth forth and weepeth, bearing precious seed, shall doubtless come again with rejoicing, bringing his sheaves with him." "Weepeth," "Doubtless," and "Rejoicing" should each have a whole line.

RUM AND MURDER.—Rev. W. D. Siegfried makes a temperance exercise by writing the word "murder" on the board, and, after talking of its terrible guilt awhile, taking the same letters he makes "Red Rum," and shows that they are *brothers* in villainy and crime.

THE LACK OF LOVE.—The Church at Ephesus was lacking in love. The following may be used: I AM SAD. Insert letters L O V E. Read: *LO*, I AM SA *VE* D. All we need to save us from our sins and our sadness is LOVE.

HAVE WE **FOUND**
HAVE WE **LOST** THE FIRST LOVE ?

THE CONSECRATED PURSE.—The following may be used in connection with the presentation of some object of benevolence: Some one proposes a new spelling for the word "personal" in the phrase "personal consecration to Christ," namely, *purse-and-all*. Some good people greatly misapprehend the full force of personal consecration. Perhaps the new style *purse-and-all* may assist in giving them a more correct conception.

MAKING SUNSHINE.—Print on the blackboard, in large letters, representing a sign

SUNSHINE FACTORY.

UNCLE JACK AND LITTLE JENNIE.

With it the following story:

"O dear! it always *does* rain when I want to go anywhere!" cried little Jennie Moore. "It's too bad! Now I've got to stay in-doors all day, and I know I shall have a wretched day."

"Perhaps so," said Uncle Jack; "but you need not have a bad day unless you choose."

"How can I help it? I wanted to go to the park and hear the band, and take Fido and play on the grass, and have a good time, and pull wild flowers and eat sandwiches under the trees; and now there isn't going to be any sunshine at all; and I'll have just time to stand here and see it rain, and see the water run off the ducks' backs."

"Well, let's make a little sunshine," said Uncle Jack.

"Make sunshine!" said Jennie; "why, how you *do* talk!" and she smiled through her tears. "You haven't got a sunshine factory, have you?"

"Well, I am going to start one right off, if you'll be my partner," replied Uncle Jack. "Now, let me give you these rules for making sunshine: First, Don't think of what might have been if the day had been better; Second, See how many pleasant things there are left to enjoy; and, Lastly, Do all you can to make other people happy."

"Well, I'll try the last thing first;" and she went to work to amuse her little brother, Willie, who was crying. By the time she had him riding a chair and laughing she was laughing too.

"Well," said Uncle Jack, "I see you are a good sunshine-maker, for you've got about all you or Willie can hold just now. But let's try what we can do with the second rule."

"But I haven't any thing to enjoy, 'cause all my dolls are old, and my picture-books all torn, and—"

"Hold," said Uncle Jack; "here's an old newspaper. Now, let's get some fun out of it."

"Fun out of a newspaper! why, how you talk!"

But Uncle Jack showed her how to make a mask by cutting holes in the paper, and how to cut a whole family of paper dolls, and how to make pretty things for Willie out of the paper. Then he got out a tea-tray, and showed her how to roll a marble round it.

And so she found many a pleasant amusement, and when bedtime came she kissed Uncle Jack and said:

"Good-night, dear Uncle Jack."

"Good-night, little sunshine-maker," said Uncle Jack.

And she dreamed that night that Uncle Jack had built a great house, and put a sign over the door which read:

SUNSHINE FACTORY.

UNCLE JACK AND LITTLE JENNIE.

She made Uncle Jack laugh when she told him her dream; but she never forgot what you must remember: A CHEERFUL HEART MAKES ITS OWN SUNSHINE.

THE ROYAL ROLL.—In simple lines, one after another, or on a large scroll, the following list of those especially mentioned with titles of divine friendship: Abraham, "The Friend of God." Benjamin, "The Beloved of God." Luke, "The Beloved Physician." John, "The Beloved Disciple." Lazarus, "Our Friend." Disciples, "My Mother and my Brethren." The Church, "The Household of God. Whosoever doeth the will of my Father,"

JESUS BROTHER, SISTER, MOTHER, I HAVE CALLED YOU FRIENDS.

HARVEST.—"He that reapeth." 1. (Daily pay) Receiveth wages. 2. (Lays up) Gathereth fruit unto life eternal. "Where hast thou gleaned to-day?" Ruth ii, 19.

The Teacher's
PREPARATION OF THE LESSON.

P	1.	PRAY.	P
R	2.	READ.	R
A	3.	COMMIT.	A
Y	4.	THINK.	Y
E	5. { CONSULT / HELPS.		E
R	6.	ADAPT.	R
	7.	ILLUSTRATE.	

"TEACH ME THY WAY, O LORD!"

This may be profitably used in teachers' meeting and institutes in suggesting a good plan for preparing the lesson. It was developed as above, in an institute at Philadelphia, by Rev. Dr. Vincent.

EMBLEMS OF CHRIST.—By *J. H. Kellogg.*—Four essential things: "A foundation—a Rock the best; Light; Bread—food; Garments—clothing."

> " Help us to build upon the *Rock;*
> Fill us, O Lord, with holy *Light;*
> Feed us, we pray, with living *Bread,*
> And clothe us all in *Garments* white."

" The Lord is my rock," 2 Sam. xxii, 2 ; " The true light," John i, 9 ; " I am the bread of life," John vi, 35 ; " Put ye on the Lord Jesus Christ," Rom. xiii, 14.

STUDY OF THE BIBLE. *Anniversary Verse Exercise.*—By *J. H. Kellogg.* Points :

1. To Read,
2. To Study,   } the Bible,
3. To Earnestly Heed,

which tells us: (1) The Truth (2) About our Saviour ; (3) Who calls us, in mercy, (4) To remember God (5) In the days of our youth.

> Yes, we will READ and STUDY the BIBLE.
> EARNESTLY HEEDING the sweet words of TRUTH ;
> And, while OUR SAVIOUR in MERCY is CALLING,
> REMEMBER our GOD in the days of our YOUTH.

The first letters spell the word " year." Shall it be in future that we do this, or now, while we have time and opportunity ? Write the word "*this*" above " year."

THE OUTCAST KING.--*Dan.* iv, 26-33.

He that humbleth himself shall be exalted.

NEBUCHADNEZZAR

EXALTED

OUT

C A S T

BY

P R I D E.

The king in the hanging gardens of Babylon. Views the great city. Heart glows with pride. He was exalted on the throne; should have been humble. He was too proud to acknowledge God. So God made the "proud prince" an "outcast." The "prodigal son," to whom the father gave his portion of the goods, too proud to stay at home. The result of pride was that PRIDE found its way among "beasts;" the perverse son fell among "swine." Read down from top, "Nebuchadnezzar exalted on the throne, outcast by pride," etc.—J. M. D

SOLOMON AND CHRIST.—Jerusalem glorious in the wealth, wisdom, power of Solomon. Heaven glorious in the riches, wisdom, dominion of the King of Kings.—*Selected.*

THE DEDICATION.—The heart of the believer the temple of the Holy Ghost. Dedicated by gifts, prayer, sacrifice. Filled with his glory. (See 2 Chron. vi, 40–42; vii, 1–5.)—*Selected.*

BIBLE CHARACTERS.—An exercise on Bible history for the infant class may be made by taking one letter after another of the alphabet and getting from them all the Bible names they can remember beginning with that letter. Other questions and stories about the persons will follow. A—Adam, Abel, Abram. B—Baal, Benjamin. C—Cain, Cornelius, etc.—J. H. V.

ANALYSIS OF THE LESSON.—We are accustomed to put an outline of the lesson on the blackboard each Sabbath, before the study of the lesson commences, in order to secure unity among the classes. We also frequently put four or five special questions below the analysis to be answered in the closing review.

BIBLE LECTURE ON UNITY OF THE BIBLE.—We give on the following page an outline for a chart or large blackboard; with smaller blackboards only a part of it can be used at once. A lecture or concert exercise may be given with it after thorough study of the history of the Bible.

UNITY OF THE BIBLE.

THE WORD OF
THE LORD
WAS UPON

AT SUNDRY TIMES.

Moses—1400 B. C.
Isaiah—750 B. C.
John—Times of Christ.
Paul—60 A. D.

STYLE.

RHET.

MANNERS

A Shepherd—Moses.
A General—Joshua.
A King—David.
A Herdsman—Amos.
A Fisherman—Peter.
A Physician—Luke.
A Tax Collector—Matthew.

"THESE ALL SPAKE WITH TONGUES
AS THE SPIRIT GAVE THEM UTTERANCE."

Chaldee—Daniel.
Hebrew—Moses, etc
Greek—Paul, etc.

"IT IS WRITTEN" FROM

The Wilderness—Moses.
The Palace—David.
The Fields—Amos, etc.
Babylon—Daniel.

Jerusalem—James.
Traveling—Luke.
Mammertine Prison—Paul.
Patmos—John.

"ALL ONE IN CHRIST JESUS."

With this division may be classed the frequent printing of parts of hymns on the board to be sung after they are used as an exercise. For example:

THE CROSS AND CROWN.

The consecrated cross I'll bear;
How long?
'Till death shall set me free.
What then?
And then go home my crown to wear,
For there's a crown for me.

3. Initial Exercise.

Next in natural order comes the Initial Exercise, by which several important words in the lesson beginning with the same letter are united together with that letter. For example:

FROM SIN TO GOD.

This exercise may be illustrated by the familiar story of Curtius and the chasm at Rome, and other stories of men who have given their lives for country or friends. Another example of this kind:

THE PRODIGAL.

R
ashness.
uin.
ebellion.
epentance.
eform.

Lost,   Sought,   Restored,
Loves,   Secured,   Rejoiced over.

Another example:

SEEKING A SAVIOUR.

STAR
SON
SAVIOUR   EEK .   AND YE SHALL FIND.
SALVATION NOWISE.

" The bright and Morning Star." *Isaiah.* " A Star shall arise out of Jacob." *Balaam.* " We have seen his star in the East." *Magi.* " Unto us a Son is given." *Isaiah.* " Son of God," " Son of Man," " Saviour of the World." " Save me." *Peter.* " Save now." *David.* Salvation to the wise now. " Him that cometh unto me I will in nowise cast out."

"Seek first the kingdom of God." "Seek for Me with all your *heart*."

SEED-THOUGHT.

DAVID'S LIFE.—He was Shepherd, Singer, Soldier, and Sovereign.

THE STRAIT GATE.—Rev. J. B. Atkinson makes an initial exercise of the following verse: "Strive to enter in at the strait gate; for many, I say unto you, will seek to enter in, and shall not be able."

THE FAITHFUL SERVANT.—Waiting, working, watching for the coming of the Lord.

THE WINGS OF THE ALMIGHTY.—Children will trust in the covert of thy wings. "How often would I have gathered thy children; .. ye would not." Illustrate this by the story of a hen who defended her chickens with great courage from the attack of a hawk, but a moment after she had killed the hawk she herself died of wounds and exhaustion. So Christ died to save us.

THE BRAZEN

The Brazen
Pointed to the
Who hath purchased
For us
And will
Us from {
And eternal

Selected.

4. THE SYLLABLE EXERCISE.

Next in natural order are those exercises in which several words are bound together by a common syllable. For example:

THE PATHWAY OF JESUS.

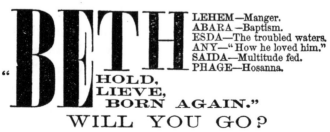

BETH LEHEM—Manger.
ABARA—Baptism.
ESDA—The troubled waters.
ANY—"How he loved him."
SAIDA—Multitude fed.
PHAGE—Hosanna.

" BE HOLD,
LIEVE,
BORN AGAIN."
WILL YOU GO?

"Behold" Jesus at Bethlehem in the manger—the Prince
of heaven wrapped in swaddling-clothes, paying the ransom
of your soul; Behold a dove descending and a voice from
heaven, at Bethlehem, saying, "This is my beloved Son;"
"Behold how he loved him" at Bethany; Behold the
cripple saved at Bethesda, the multitude fed at Bethsaida;
"Behold thy king cometh (from Bethphage) amid palms and
hosannas." Believe in this Christ and you shall be "born
again," and have a Christmas and Bethlehem in your own
heart; you shall be *baptized* into Christ, raised from the death
of sin, fed with angels' food, and your heart filled with "Hosannas." "*Will you go*" in this pathway with Jesus?

SEED-THOUGHT.

RE.—At our teachers' meeting, on Tuesday evening, Mr.
Wisener, the superintendent, gave us a little lecture on
teaching. He placed the above syllable on the blackboard,
and by six additions gave us six rules for our preparation.
"So teach," said he, "that the minds you work upon will

"1. RE-CEIVE the truth into intellect, conscience, and affections.

"2. RE-TAIN the truth, this being made easy through the
comprehensive and condensed forms in which you communicate it.

"3. RE-CUR to the truth frequently, having been charmed by
it, and being by its apt illustrations constantly reminded
of it.

"4. RE-FLECT on the truth, thus making it a quickener of
the intellect, and from the seed you hold in the mind you
will produce other truths.

"5. RE-FORM by the truth, it being accompanied by the
Holy Ghost in the processes of regeneration and sanctifi-
cation.

"6. RE-COMMUNICATE the truth. He is never well taught
who cannot re-port or re-teach the truth he has received."

This was the substance of Mr. Wisener's lecture. It was aptly illustrated, and we passed him a vote of thanks.

ONE OF THE TEACHERS.

THE FOE AND FRIEND.—*By Rev. J. M. Durrell.*

SATANVIOUR SEDcDUCCURES US UNTOUNTO US DEATH.LIFE.

CAUSING

REMORSELIEF EVERLASTING.MORE.

5. THE WORD EXERCISE.

This class includes exercises, in which two or more passages or statements are bound together by a common word. For example:

WHAT WILL YOU HAVE?—(See Prov. xxiii, 29.)

THEY THAT TARRY LONG AT THE SEEK MIXED WINE,

WHAT WILL YOU HAVE?
BABBLINGS.
REDNESS OF EYES.
CONTENTIONS.
WOUNDS.
SORROW.
WOE.

SAMPLE ROOM.

The words "What will you—(have)" are not to be written until after all the others have been written and spoken of. Illustrations for this exercise may be taken from the following

"Specimens of the Work Done Inside."

A young man in prison had such a strong thirst for intoxicating liquor that he cut off his hand at the wrist, called for a bowl of brandy in order to stop the bleeding, thrust his wrist into the bowl, and then drank the contents.

A wife was dangerously sick and her husband went for her medicine. On the way home he stopped to drink with a friend; one glass led to others; after a long time he came home stupefied with drink, and threw himself upon the bed where the helpless wife was lying in mortal agony. He woke at midnight, startled by a terrible thunder-storm that was raging, and found his wife cold in death at his side.

In a village near Boston, an old man, the slave of appetite, endeavored to get some liquor as a medicine, being unable to get it as a drink. He said he needed it on account of trouble with his feet. Being suspected, he was told he could use it in the drug-store, but could not carry it away. He poured it into his boots, and was seen a few minutes later behind a fence, greedily drinking the liquor from his boots.

Nay, more, a slave of this habit, unable to buy any liquor, stole and drank the spirits with which a corpse had been bathed a few hours before!

Blacker yet was the act of those rum-thirsty sailors who tapped the barrel in which a dead animal was being preserved, and greedily drank the liquor to satisfy their burning appetite.

A man who had broken the heart of his wife by his drunken abuse stood by her bedside in her last sickness. She made him most solemnly promise never to take liquor again except he should receive it from her hand. After she had died, maddened by appetite, he poured out the glass for which he thirsted, and placing his wife's cold fingers around the glass, took the drink from her lifeless hand.

We give another example of this class:

"THE VOICE OF GOD IS UPON THE WATERS:"

"BE STILL AND KNOW THAT

I AM GOD."

JESUS ~~Talking to~~ ~~Taking money from~~ ~~Calming~~ ~~Walking on~~ ~~Filling nets from~~ THE SEA.

JESUS Slept upon Rebuked the Wind and THE SEA—"Surely He hath borne our griefs."—"Truly this was the Son of God."

The incidents connected with the Sea of Galilee should be thoroughly looked up, and then this exercise may be used very impressively to exhibit the humanity and divinity of Christ, who wearily walked the sands of the shore as a man, and then triumphantly walked on its waves as a God; who gratified his hunger at the fisherman's table, but fed five thousand at once by miraculous power; who submitted as a man to the tax collector, but took the money as a God from a fish of the sea; who asked the disciples in regard to their thoughts, but soon after heard the words "Thou knowest all things."

He slept as the son of man on a sailor's pillow, but rose as the Son of God to still the storm with a word. As we look at one side of the picture we say, "Surely he hath borne our griefs." As we turn to the other we cry, "Truly this was the Son of God."

SEED-THOUGHT.

TOTAL ABSTINENCE.—Several other temperance exercises may be made as follows, using the excuses: "Just here," "Just once," "Just a drop," "Just one glass," "For the bride's sake," "For health's sake," "For the country's sake," etc.

Rev. W. D. Siegfried has made a temperance alphabet, with which we connect a word exercise at the close. A-le and alcohol, B-eer and brandy, C-ider and champagne, D-runk-ard, E-nslaved, F-orsaken, G-rave, H-ell, and

Froth— ⌈ CAN
Dregs— ⌊ WOULD   **ABSTAIN, BUT I**   WONT.
CANT.

The following, clipped from a newspaper, will suggest a word exercise with the word *loss:*

THE LOSSES RESULTING FROM STRONG DRINK.

"Loss of money; loss of time; loss of health; loss of business; loss of character; loss of friends; loss of good conscience; loss of feeling; loss of mind; loss of life; loss of the *immortal soul.*"

SELFISHNESS AND PRIDE.—The Pharisee's prayer in which he uses "I" very often, and the rich man who said, "I have much goods," and often used "I" and "MY," will suggest word exercises to group about "I" and "my," representing strikingly self-love and self-sufficiency. Peter also at the Passover uses "I" frequently, but on the shores of Galilee, after his denial, "thou" takes the place of "I" at the beginning and end of his sentences.

THE MODEL SCHOLAR.—(Jesus at twelve years. Luke i, 40, etc.)

Obedient to God, to his parents. Diligent in questioning, in learning. Inquiring in God's house, of good men. Searching the Scriptures. Some picture of the Scriptures in rolls as they were at that time, or a picture of the temple or of the doctors of the law, may well be shown with this exercise. The story itself is very dramatic. The boy among old and learned men—the anxious parents—the journey. Each item, vividly described, is full of interest.—*Selected.*

JESUS SAYS:

Righteous
Holy
My   **FATHER**   —FEAR—SINAI.
—Orphanage.
OUR   —LOVE—OLIVET.

When Jesus says " *Righteous* Father," or *Holy* Father," it only suggests fear and the terrors of Sinai's justice; when he says " *My* Father," it only reminds us of our own orphanage; but when he says " Our Father," it lifts us to the Olivet of love, and reminds us that in Christ we have an " elder Brother."

" I remember," says Dr. Fowler, " once standing by the surging billows all one weary day, and watching for hours a father struggling beyond in the breakers for the life of his son. They came slowly toward the breakers on a piece of wreck, and as they came the waves turned over the piece of float, and they were lost. Presently we saw the father come to the surface and clamber alone to the wreck, and then saw him plunge off into the waves, and thought he was gone; but in a moment he came back again, holding his boy. Presently they struck another wave, and over they went; and again they repeated the process. Again they went over, and again the father rescued his son. By and by, as they swung nearer the shore, they caught on a snag just out beyond where we could reach them, and for a little time the waves went over them there till we saw the boy in the father's arms, hanging down in helplessness, and knew they must be saved soon or be lost. I shall never forget the gaze of that father. And as we drew him from the devouring waves, still clinging to his son, he said, ' That's my boy, that's my boy!' and half frantic, as we dragged them up the bank, he cried all the time, ' That's my boy, that's my boy!'. And so I have thought, in hours of darkness, when the billows roll over me, the great Father is reaching down to me, and, taking hold of me, crying, ' That's my boy!' and I know I am safe."

THE BRAVE YOUNG MEN.—Dan. iii, 13–18.—By *Rev. J. M. Durrell.*

WE WILL NOT SERVE YOUR GODS,
THEY ARE WILL NOT ABLE TO DELIVER US,
FIGHT FOR US.

Let "we," "your gods," "they are able to," "us," and "will," be on the board.

Begin by asking what courage is: not natural timidity, but a *will* to do *right*, even though we dread the danger that may *seem* to result. Napoleon said of one of his troopers who was naturally timid, but who with compressed lips was marching up to the enemy's line with a firm tread, "That man is brave; he realizes the danger, but faces it." Then write "Will" on the blackboard. State that courage consists of two parts: will *not* to do wrong, and will to do right. Daniel and his companions had the first; they said, "We will *not* serve thy gods." Write "Not serve," and speak of the importance of saying "no" at the right time. Boy on street, looked into a liquor saloon where some one was playing on a violin; fond of music; keeper saw him standing on sidewalk; invited him in; boy replied "*No;* my mother told me never to have any thing to do with men who sell rum."

People of Babylon worshiped more than one God; gods, all together, not able to deliver us, nor fight for us. Write "Deliver" and "fight for." The priests of Baal unable to secure answer from them on the mount with Elijah.

Daniel and friends not only said *no* to wrong, but *yes* to right; had courage to worship god in the face of danger. Opposed to the gods of Babylon was the one God of heaven and earth. Erase the *y* and *s* of "your gods," so as to read "our God." Erase "not," the *t* and *y* of "they," cancel "are" with "is," and the exercise reads, "We will serve our God; he is able to deliver us; he will fight for us." "Wait on the Lord; be of good courage, and he shall strengthen thine heart; wait, I say, on the Lord." Psa. xxvii, 14.

SUCCESS.—Take the two passages, Eccl. ii, 3 (a part of the verse as a question) and Micah vi, 8. Print, in large letters, "GOOD;" at its right print the words, "What is that (good)?" Then write below, one answer after another, 1. Wealth; 2. Fame; 3. Pleasure; 4. Power; and show that each of these is unsatisfactory. Put a "*not*" before them or over them. Then write God's answer. Above the word "Good" write, "He hath showed thee, a man, what is ———," and below, opposite to wealth, fame, etc., write, 1. Do justly; 2. Love mercy; 3. Walk humbly with God.

LOVE, JOY, PEACE, ETC.—The Bible abounds in passages containing "Love," "Joy," "Peace," "Trust," and other words in regard to inward life; also in passages containing "Watch," "Work," "Fight," and other words belonging to the outward life, and whenever any one of these words is to be spoken of, the memory or Concordance will at once furnish a word exercise.

THE LORD'S PRAYER.

OUR FATHER

THY
Name—Be Hallowed.
Kingdom—Come.
Will—Be Done.

FOR GIVE
LEAD
DELIVER
US F O R WE ARE Needy. Sinful.
WANDER.
ARE IN DANGER.

THINE
KINGDOM, POWER, GLORY,
FOREVER,
AMEN."   *Matt.* vi, 9–13.

6. PHRASE EXERCISE.

This class comprises those exercises in which a common phrase binds together several passages. For example:

ELISHA'S DEFENDERS.—2 *Kings* vi, 16.

"THE LORD OF HOSTS IS
"THEY THAT BE   WITH US

ARE MORE THAN THEY
THAT BE
WITH THEM."

"IF GOD BE FOR US
WHO CAN BE AGAINST US?"

When London was shaken with the great earthquake, and houses were falling on every side; when the ground rocked like the sea in a storm, and men cried for mercy, thinking the end of all things had come, Wesley gathered his little band of Christians in their chapel and read calmly to them, as they responded in many a deep and fervent amen, the Forty-sixth Psalm: " God is our refuge and strength, a very present help in trouble. Therefore will not we fear, though the earth be removed," etc.

" THE MAIDEN MARTYR OF SCOTLAND " was tied to a stake on the Scottish beach at low tide, because she would not recant her faith in Christ. Below her another Christian was placed, that the maiden might be intimidated into recanting by the sight of another's death agony.

Again and again they offered to unbind her, as the tide rose about her, if she would give up her religion.

Her only answer was prayer to God for strength. Then when the cold waters had risen high about her she began to sing the hymn,

" O Thou, from whom all goodness flows,
I lift my soul to Thee," etc.,

and sang until the waters closed her lips, and her spirit floated out into eternity.

A good man who had long loved God was sick, the worst of all sickness, a sick mind—full of sorrow, tired of life, and hardly knowing what a terrible thing he was going to do, got into a carriage, told the driver to go to a river bank and leave him there. He meant, when he was alone, to drown himself in the dark deep river. But God would not let his dear sick child do so wicked a thing; after a time the horses stopped, and looking up he was back at his own house. The driver did not guide them right, and they went back home. He got out, went in and wrote this hymn, which every child should learn ·

"God moves in a mysterious way."

The expression "*The Lord was with* ——" is associated with Joseph, Moses, Daniel, David, etc. These also may be grouped into a phrase exercise, and the application made to the passage "The Lord of hosts is with us." In the pit where Joseph was cast, the basket-cradle of Moses, the den of lions, and the other places of trial in the lives of those mentioned, God was with them.

THE TONGUE.—Four sins of the tongue are prohibited with the words "*Thou shalt not*," and may be grouped together as above: " Ye shall not lie one to another;" "Ye shall not swear by my name falsely;" "Ye shall not profane the name of thy God;" "Ye shall not go up and down as a talebearer." The following penalties may be written or mentioned in connection with this exercise: 1. LIES. "He that telleth lies shall not tarry in my sight." 2. FALSE SWEARING: "Shall not enter the kingdom of heaven." 3. PROFANITY: "The Lord will not hold him guiltless." 4. TALEBEARING: "Him will I cut off." Below it all the motto, "Sinned not with his tongue."

THINK.—The phrases "I didn't think" and "Don't forget" will bind in two groups the following suggestive exercises and precepts: "I didn't think it was wrong;" "I didn't think it would do any harm;" "I didn't think it would hurt me to smoke;" "I didn't think I should ever be a drunkard;" "I didn't think I should lose my soul." Don't forget that you are a sinner; don't forget that you are in danger; don't forget that you must give an account; don't forget that you must live forever; don't forget that you may be saved; don't forget that you must be saved or lost. Below write, "Whatsoever things are * true, * honest, * just, * pure, * lovely, * think on these things." Illustrate with this incident:

A young man who had been putting off the subject of religion was one day thrown from his horse and carried into the nearest house, and, being told that he could not live an hour, cried out, "Must I go into eternity in an hour? Must I stand before my Judge in one short hour? God knows I have made no preparation for this event! I have heard of impenitent young men thus suddenly cut off, but it never occurred to me that I should be one! O tell me, tell me what I must do to be saved!" He was told that he must repent of his sins, and look to Jesus Christ for pardon. "But I do not know *how* to repent. The whole work of my life-time is crowded into this hour of agony. O what shall I do to be saved?" he continued to cry with an eye glaring with desperation. But death would not wait for "explanations," and thus crying out for aid and instruction he sank back upon his pillow, and in another moment was in eternity.

DARKNESS AND LIGHT.—"The blind sent to Siloam to wash and receive sight;" "The sinful sent to the Saviour to wash and be saved;" "I went, washed, received sight;" "I obeyed, trusted, am saved;" "ONCE BLIND, NOW I SEE." Said a preacher to a young lady, "How were you converted?" "I went to God, believed his word, and was saved." "*As they went they were cleansed.*"

LOYALTY IN ALL THINGS.—The familiar motto may be put on the board as a phrase exercise: "Do all the good you can; at all times you can; in all the ways you can; to all the people you can; as long as ever you can." The words "all you can" are the common phrase to be printed large. On this same subject are the passages, "I will follow thee whithersoever thou goest," (spoken on earth,) and "These are they that follow the Lamb whithersoever he goeth," (spoken in heaven;) also the passages, "Whether we live we live unto the Lord, or whether we die, we die unto the Lord; whether we live, therefore, or die we are the Lord's." It will be enough, perhaps, to put on the board simply "live," "die," "unto the Lord."

GIVE ME DRINK.—The following may be impressively grouped around the phrase "Give me drink:"

Mr. M'Leod, an English writer, puts the following language in the mouths of those who visit the rumseller's den:

"There's my money—give me drink! There's my clothing and food and fire of my wife and children—give me drink! There's the education of my family and the peace of the house—give me drink! There's the rent I have robbed from my landlord, fees I have robbed from my schoolmaster, and innumerable articles I have robbed from the shopkeeper—give me drink! Pour me out drink for yet more, I will pay for it! There's my health of body and peace of mind; there's my character as a man and my profession as a Christian; I give up all—give me drink! More yet have I to give! There's my heavenly inheritance and the eternal friendship of the redeemed; there, there is all hope of salvation! I give up my Saviour! I give up my God! I give up all that is great, good, and glorious in the universe! I resign all forever, that I may be drunk!"

7. Table Exercise.

This class comprises those exercises in which several passages or thoughts are grouped into some sort of a table. For example:

Blessing and Cursing.—Having told the school to find in the Bible, during the previous week, six things that God hates, and eight things that God blesses, hinting, if necessary, that somewhere in Proverbs and Matthew the information may be found, put on the board, before the opening of the school, what is below except the words which follow the figures in each row. These should be drawn from the school by questions, when the blackboard exercise is explained, near the close of the session:

THUS SAITH THE LORD:

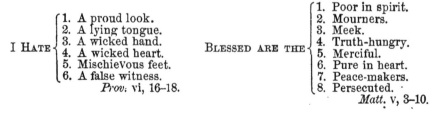

I Hate
1. A proud look.
2. A lying tongue.
3. A wicked hand.
4. A wicked heart.
5. Mischievous feet.
6. A false witness.
    Prov. vi, 16–18.

Blessed are the
1. Poor in spirit.
2. Mourners.
3. Meek.
4. Truth-hungry.
5. Merciful.
6. Pure in heart.
7. Peace-makers.
8. Persecuted.
    Matt. v, 3–10.

Below the first group write, "They shall call on the rocks and hills to hide them from the wrath of the Lamb." Under the other, "These are they that follow the Lamb whithersoever he goeth."

The first verses of the First Psalm may be used *above* these groups at the close, giving the *present* condition of things, as the passages below give the *future:*   •

"BLESSED

Is the man that walketh

NOT	BUT
In the Counsel	His delight is
of the	in the
Ungodly,	Law of the Lord."
(Those things hated.) ·	(Those things blessed.)

GOSPEL IDEA OF A MAN.

	Faith.
	Virtue.
	Knowledge.
(" Add.")	Temperance.
	Brotherly Kindness.
	Charity.

Total—A TRUE MAN.

God is not satisfied with pet virtues; with good temperance men who have no brotherly kindness; with faith in those who have not charity; with virtue, but not according to knowledge. We are to " *add* " these together, having the faith that mounts up on wings as eagles, the virtue that shall run and not be weary, the patience that shall walk and not faint, the brotherly kindness that beareth all things, and the charity that never faileth.

The following example was suggested by an exercise of Rev. Dr. M'Cook:

Christ on the shores of Galilee makes five loaves into five thousand loaves by a *touch*. God gives us our daily bread by means of the long process, " Seed, germ, stalk," etc. The result is the same in either case, "We are fed." Surely, then, "Christ is God." Other miracles of Christ may thus be compared with works of God to show his oneness in power with the Father.

GOD'S GIFTS.—(By *Rev. A. L. Bruce.*

SEEK YE FIRST———	The Kingdom of God.
	Riches.
" ALL THESE	Honor.
THINGS	Happiness.
SHALL	Peace.
BE	Prosperity.
ADDED	Food.
UNTO	Length of Days.
YOU."	Victory in Death.
	Eternal Life.

" ALL THINGS ARE YOURS."

With the words, " Riches, honor," etc., use the following proof-texts: " The blessing of the Lord it maketh rich;" "He shall stand before kings;" "My cup runneth over," "Great peace have they;" "The righteous shall flourish as the palm tree;" "Verily thou shalt be fed;" "With long life will I satisfy him;" "Thanks be unto God who giveth us the victory;" "Enter thou into the joy of thy Lord."

THE WONDERFUL—Luke vii, 18–23.

"THE WORKS OF MY FATHER."

Blind		See.
Lame		Walk.
Lepers	AT THE **WORD** of **JESUS.**	Cleansed.
Deaf		Hear.
Dead		Live again.

GLAD TIDINGS TO THE. POOR.

"Thou hast given him power over all flesh."

Selected.

PROGRESS OF THE WICKED.—(By *Rev. W. J. Gladwin.*)

Psa. i, 1.

"Blessed is the man that

	A.	B.	C.
1.	WALKETH not in	the COUNSEL of the	UNGODLY nor
2.	STANDETH in	the WAY of	SINNERS nor
3.	SITTETH in	the SEAT of	the SCORNFUL."

I. Notice the progress in each column.

II. Find proof-texts and examples. Thus, the example of Peter:

1. WALKETH : "Followed afar off." Luke xxii, 54.
2. STANDETH : "Stood and warmed himself." John xviii, 25. 3. SITTETH : "Sat down among them." Luke xxii, 55.

III. How far are *you* in this road ? How about that *pride ?* ill temper ? etc.

There are two ways of coming down from the top of a church steeple—one is to jump down, and the other is to come down by the steps; but both will lead you to the bottom. So also there are two ways of leading you to hell: one is to walk into it with your eyes open—few people do that—the other is to go down by the steps of *little sins*, and that way, I fear, is only too common. Put up with a few little sins, and you will soon want a few more, and your course will be regularly worse every day. Even a heathen could say, "Who was content with only one sin?" Well did Jeremy Taylor describe the progress of sin in man: "First it startles him, then it becomes pleasing, then easy, then delightful, then frequent, then habitual, then confirmed. Then the man is impenitent, then obstinate, and then he is damned." Reader, the devil only wants to get the wedge of a little allowed sin into your heart, and you will soon be all his own! Never play with the fire—never trifle with little sins."

The history of Eve's sin, and also of Cain's crime, will illustrate these downward steps:

EVE { Saw, Took, Ate, Gave.   CAIN { Very wroth, Talked, Rose against Abel, Slew him.

We first look upon sin, then think of it, touch it, taste it, and then drag others down with ourselves. So the sin of Gehazi also began with a thought; for when Gehazi "said," etc., he said it to himself—there was, therefore, nothing but a thought at the beginning. Trace the gradation—thought, first; next, "run after him;" next, "take somewhat." Show how thieving and bold robbery begins and ends. Every sin goes by gradation. You will find it so in the lesson. Note, also, the increasing determination: first, the mere thought unfavorable to the expediency of the act of generosity, so far as his master was concerned; next, in determining what he would do, ending all in an irreverent oath, using the name of Jehovah—it was the latter word which he pronounced, in direct violation of one of the commandments. Point: All sin begins feebly, but has a tendency to end in power—begins in thought, ends in act. Hence, evil thoughts to be guarded against.

CHRIST CLEANSING THE TEMPLE.

THE LORD IS IN HIS HOLY

TEMPLE.   PSA. xi, 4.

For the Superintendent's review reverse the board, and, after a few preliminary words regarding the Passover, ask, Into what building did Jesus go? Write *Temple*, as in diagram.

. **TEMPLE.**

$$\text{MEN SELLING} \begin{cases} \text{OXEN,} \\ \text{SHEEP,} \\ \text{DOVES.} \end{cases}$$

MONEY CHANGERS.

——

HEART.

SELFISHNESS,	BOASTING,
COVETOUSNESS,	LYING,
PRIDE,	INGRATITUDE,
BLASPHEMY,	ENVY.

Take these things Hence.

M. T. Bailey.

THE CHRISTIAN'S INHERITANCE.

"ALL THINGS

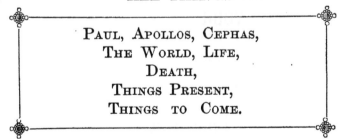

PAUL, APOLLOS, CEPHAS,
THE WORLD, LIFE,
DEATH,
THINGS PRESENT,
THINGS TO COME.

ARE YOURS,
AND YE ARE CHRIST'S, GOD'S."
AND

8. The Acrostic Exercise.

The acrostic exercise binds several passages or points together by their initial letters being formed into the important word of the lesson or address.   For example:

Jesus in the Temple.

OUR   ound,

RGUING,

EMPLE,

OW THAT YE $\begin{cases} \text{left us ?} \\ \text{sought me ?} \end{cases}$

ETURNED.

The word "Our" and the acrostic letters "Father" in red, and the rest in white.

Watchfulness.

WATCH
YOUR
Words,
Actions,
Thoughts,
Company.
Hearts.   *J. H. Watt.*

"SEARCH THE SCRIPTURES." (John v, 39.)

SEARCH THE
SCRIPTURES

EARNESTLY,

ANXIOUSLY,

REGULARLY,

CAREFULLY,   Heb. xii, 17.

HUMBLY.   *S. W. C.*

"HOW SHALL I WORK?"

L OOKING to Jesus.
O rderly.
V aliantly.
I n hope.
N ever doubting.
G lorifying God.
L iving near the Cross.
Y ielding all to Christ.   *J. B. Phipps.*

GIVING TO GOD.

1. HOW {
    re **G** ularly,
    will **I** ngly,
    de **V** outly,
    lib **E** rally,

UNTO THE

2. WHY {
    L oves the giver,
    O rdains the possession
    R ewards the act,
    D emands the duty.

S. S. Times.

JESUS THE GREAT TEACHER.   (John vii, 40–46.)

"NEVER MAN

JESUS $\Big\{$
E

MAN."
Selected.

THE TWO MASTERS.   (1 John iii, 8.)

THE WORK OF

DECEIVES,	**J**USTIFIES,
ENTICES,	**E**LEVATES
VITIATES,	**S**ANCTIFIES
INFATUATES,	**U**NITES TO GOD,
LEADS TO HELL.	**S**AVES.

S. U. M., St. Louis, Mo.

THE CRUCIFIXION.

"THEY CRUCIFIED HIM."   (Matt. xxvii, 35.)

A	**C** ruel
A	**R** ighteous
An	**U** nrepentant
A   Thorn-**C** rowned
An	**I** nnocent
The	**F** aithful
The	**I** nhuman
An	**E** arnest
A	**D** ivine

Kellogg.

"FOLLOW ME." (Luke ix 51–62.)

FOLLOW

ME,

ONSTANTLY,

UMBLY,

EVERENTLY,

MMEDIATELY.

To HEAR,
OBEY,
IMITATE.

UPREMELY,

RUSTINGLY.

Fred. C. Elliott.

9. PARALLEL AND CONTRAST EXERCISES.

This division includes those exercises where different passages or thoughts are arranged to parallel or contrast with each other to show similarity or antitheses.

It is useful to set before a school " life and death, blessing and cursing," to bring out the contrasts in the life of Christ and in Christian character, etc.

THE TWO TEMPTATIONS.

EDEN.	WILDERNESS.
THE FIRST ADAM.	THE SECOND ADAM.
1. EAT—	1. EAT—
2. YE SHALL BE AS GODS.	2. ALL THESE KINGDOMS.
3. YE SHALL NOT SURELY DIE.	3. CAST THYSELF DOWN.
"I hid myself."	"Get thee behind me."

ANGELS CAME AND

DROVE HIM FORTH.   MINISTERED UNTO HIM.

Satan is the same shrewd tempter in the wilderness as in Eden. He first tries *appetite*, then *ambition*, and then *perverts the word of God.* The father of lies said to Adam, " Ye shall be as gods." See him who was to be " as gods " sneaking in the bushes. He said to Christ, " I will give you all the kingdoms of the world," when he did not own enough to rest his foot on. Temptation comes to-day, first to *appetite ;* then, for the power of wealth or fame, we are urged to wrong-doing ; then we are tempted to " cast ourselves down " into soul-dangers, and even into eternity unprepared, and trust to God's angels. Cancel the three temptations with "*It is written.*"

THE TRUE GENTLEMAN. (1 Cor. xiii.)

"SHOW YOURSELVES MEN."

[Front.]   [Reverse.]

(*The World's Requirements.*)   (*God's Requirements.*)

BY	Smoking,	A TRUE GENTLEMAN
	Swearing,	is kind,
	Drinking,	envieth not,
	Dressing,	vaunteth not,
	Pride,	is not puffed up,
	Politeness,	doth not behave unseemly,
		seeketh not his own,
	HAVING	is not easily provoked,
		thinketh no evil,
	Eloquence,	rejoiceth,
	Knowledge,	beareth,
	Generosity,	believeth,
	Sacrifice. (1 *Cor.* xiii, 1.)	endureth.

TOTAL—"I AM NOTHING."   TOTAL—"NEVER FAILETH."

After discussing "the world's requirements" on the front of the blackboard, print over it all "Sounding brass and tinkling cymbal." Then turn the blackboard, and show how perfectly the thirteenth chapter of first Corinthians describes the true gentleman.

DANIEL'S TEMPERANCE SOCIETY. (Dan. i, 8–17.)

RECORDS
OF

A Temperance Society.   A Wine Club.

ORGANIZATION.

PRES....................Daniel.	PRES.............King Darius.
Members { ....Hananiah. ....Mishael. ....Azariah.	Members :
	ALL THE KINGDOM.

AFTER TEN DAYS' WORKING.

FAIRER, FATTER IN FLESH.   NO IMPROVEMENT.

Rev. J. M. Durrell.

Well to compare the effects of temperance societies and wine clubs. A thing tested by its practical working. Draw out of school the organization of the two societies, and put on board as the answers are obtained. After ten days' working· Alcohol a poison; speak of its effects on body. When, in 1832, the cholera raged in Montreal, of 1,200 cases not a drunkard recovered. In Russia, of 2,160 cases in twenty-one days, drunkards all died. In Glasgow, when patients were treated with alcoholic medicines, one in five died. Now that alcohol is abolished, one in forty die. After three years: Draw out answers, and put on board as before. Temperance is good for mind. Rum makes idiots. Decision of the king, the president of the wine-club. Four temperance, etc. One man with a clear head better than one hundred with dull ones. These four were *Christian* temperance men. The temple of total abstinence must be built upon the Rock, Christ—"Our Rock," etc. Which society will you join?

SKEPTICISM.

Is there a God
Have I a soul
Can Christ save
Is there any Holy Ghost
May I be a Christian
Is there a heaven

FAITH.

"Abba, Father"
"God in us"
"Jesus saves me"
"The Spirit witnesseth"
"Whosoever" means me
"By faith I can see it afar"

Skeptics live always with an interrogation mark on them; reason cuts off the top and leaves the period of fact; exultant faith has climbed higher, and shouts its confidence in exclamations of joy.

THE FRIEND AT MIDNIGHT. (Luke xi, 5–13.)

ASK	SEEK	KNOCK AT
THE LIGHT	THE WAY	THE DOOR
	ASK	
GIVEN	FOUND	OPENED.

S. W. C.

THE PHARISEE AND PUBLICAN. (Luke xviii, 9–14.)

VAIN   TRUE

PRAYER

I AM JUST.
FAST.
GIVE TITHES.   God { BE MERCIFUL
TO ME
A SINNER.

BROKEN IN HEART.   *S. W. C.*

The following striking resemblances *between* the acts of God the Father and God the Son may be used, a part at a time, for several exercises on the Divinity of Christ.

"THE FATHER WORKETH HITHERTO, AND I WORK."

GOD   **CHRIST**

GAVE

LAW ON SINAI.   GOLDEN RULE ON OLIVET.

COMMISSIONED

MOSES   DISCIPLES

ON

HOREB.   MOUNT OF ASCENSION.

CLOSED

MOUTHS OF THE LIONS.   EYES OF THE NAZARENES.

UNHARMED

D A N I E L   J E S U S

Shadrach, Meshach, and Abednego

SAFE THROUGH

FURNACE.   MOB.

CHANGED

BITTER TO SWEET.   WATER TO WINE.

FED

ISRAELITES   THE MULTITUDE

IN THE WILDERNESS.

" BREATHED

INTO MAN'S NOSTRILS   ON HIS DISCIPLES, saying,

RECEIVE YE

THE BREATH OF LIFE."   THE HOLY GHOST."

"Whatsoever doeth the Father, that doeth the Son likewise."

The Endless Sabbath.

CREATION—God
LIFE—The Christian
WORK^{ED—"Very Good"}—REST { EVER-
_{S —"Well Done"} { MORE.

"WORK while the day is shining,
There's RESTING by and by."

When God had finished his work, and found it "very good," he began his endless Sabbath. When we have finished our work, and heard the Father's "Well done," our rest begins. *Work* through the little while; *rest* through the "evermore."

The Multiplication Table of Forgiveness.

PETER— 7 times 1 }
CHRIST—7 times 70 } "Charity never faileth."
Matt. xviii, 21, 22.

The Lesser of Two Evils. (Matt. xviii, 6.)

Lightest.	Heaviest.
(Outline of a Millstone.)	"Offend one of these Little Ones."
"SEA."	"HELL."

WEIGHED IN GOD'S BALANCES.

On Matt. vi, 1–6.

The following is given by W. H. Sutton. Our blackboard said to all who came in:

GOD LOOKS AT OUR HEARTS.

After the class-study the board was turned over. The school found the following:

The
CHRISTIAN | HYPOCRITE.
Gives and Prays
to be
Seen and Heard
by
——— | ———

The scholars themselves supplied the blanks, and we placed on the right-hand side blank the word MAN, on the left, GOD.

"LIKE HIM, FOR WE SHALL SEE HIM AS HE IS."

STEPHEN.
"Lay not this sin to their charge."

SAUL.
"Lord, what wilt thou have me to DO?"

CHRIST.

" Father, forgive them."

" I come to DO the will of him that sent me."

"WHEREFORE are they before the throne."

God hath highly exalted him."

Saul *saw* Christ at the gate of Damascus, Stephen at the gate of Jerusalem; and even by that brief glance they seem to have caught something of his spirit, as their words indicate.

BODY AND SOUL

The Body.

"FARED SUMPTUOUSLY,"
"IN PURPLE AND FINE LINEN,"
"ENOUGH AND TO SPARE,"
A PALACE,

And yet MORTAL.

THE KING OF GLORY.

ON EARTH.	IN HEAVEN.
LOWLY,	EXALTED,
DESPISED,	ADORED,
SERVANT,	KING,
CONDEMNED,	JUDGE,
SUFFERING.	**GLORY.**

THE PASCHAL FEAST. (Exod. xii, 11–15.)

ANGEL OF DEATH.

LAMB.

ISRAELITES

SAVED BY THE BLOOD,
STRENGTHENED BY THE FLESH,
STANDING, READY TO DEPART.

EGYPTIANS

Slain ! ! !

A *lamb* between the Angel of Death and the homes of the Israelites saved them. No such shield for the Egyptians.

So Christ, the Lamb of God, is our salvation. His blood saves, (1 John i, 7;) his flesh is "meat indeed," (John vi, 54, 55 ;) and while we partake we are strangers and pilgrims ready for departure. (1 Pet. ii, 11.)

EVERY PROMISE CONDITIONAL.

CONDITION.	PROMISE.
Ask,	Receive.
Seek,	Find.
Knock,	Opened.
Come,	Rest.
Stayed on thee,	Kept in peace.
Draw nigh to God,	He will draw nigh.
Commit thy ways unto the Lord,	He will direct thy paths.
If ye faint not,	Ye shall reap.
Faithful unto death,	Crown of life.

"FAITHFUL IS HE THAT HATH PROMISED, WHO ALSO WILL DO IT."

CONTRASTS IN PETER'S EXPERIENCE.

PASSOVER—**MEAL**—"I WILL FOLLOW THEE."
SEASIDE— —"THOU KNOWEST THAT I LOVE THEE."

PILATE'S HALL—**FIRE**—"Warmed himself."
SEASIDE— —Walked with Jesus.

PILATE'S—**COURT**—"I know not the man."
ANNAS'S— —"Whether it be right in the sight of God to hearken unto you more than unto God, judge ye."

GETHSEMANE—**SLEEP**—Indifference.
JOPPA— —Prejudice.
PRISON— —TRUST.

Peter had a wonderful change in his character from boastfulness to humility, from selfishness to Christlikeness, from indifference to trustfulness. Fickle in his promise at the Passover *meal*, humble at the *meal* by the fire of coals—"I" has changed to "Thou;" selfish by the court fire, walking with Jesus from the seaside fire; cowardly in the court-room of Pilate, and courageous in the court-room where he was charged not to speak at all or to teach in this name ; sleeping

8

with *indifference* in the garden, with prejudice on the house-top, with trust in the prison. He visited the mount: "It is good for us to be here;" but he learned to *dwell* on the mount of trust.

10. CANCELING EXERCISE.

Very many impressive exercises may be made by canceling a word or sentence with a better or brighter one. For example:

THE PRE-EMINENCE OF JESUS. AT THE TRANSFIGURATION.

    1. LAW—MOSES.
    2. PROPHETS—ELIAS.
    3. GOSPELS—JOHN.
    4. EPISTLES—PETER AND JAMES.

Write in some brightly-colored chalk, "HEAR YE HIM" over the first row, after talking about it as it stands; then write "JESUS ONLY" over the other row.

Instead of the books we shall see "Hear ye him;" instead of the men, "Jesus only." As we look upon the mount, Peter and James and John are on their faces; Moses and Elias have faded out in the brightness of Christ's glory, and we "*see no man save Jesus only.*" Below the above exercise print as follows:

LOOK NOT TO ' WHAT THEY THINK."
HEAR NOT WHAT THEY DO."
                                              SAY."

Write in red chalk, over the parts opposite "Look," the following, to cancel the error, "to JESUS ONLY." So, after "HEAR," the following, "YE HIM."

First, the exercise standing as it is above, show how we measure and plan by those strange yard-sticks and mirrors "What they *think*" and "What *they do*." and how we always have a hand to the ear for "What *they say*." Then cancel these errors, and let the revised exercise read, "LOOK TO JESUS ONLY"—"HEAR YE HIM."

How to be Saved.

BY GREAT $\begin{smallmatrix}\text{URBAN}\\\text{MORAL}\\\text{CHAR}\end{smallmatrix}$ ITY $\begin{smallmatrix}\text{ARE}\\\text{YE}\end{smallmatrix}$ SAVED,

THROUGH

$\text{F}\begin{smallmatrix}\text{ORTUNATE CIRCUMSTANCES.}\\\text{AVORED DISPOSITIONS.}\\\text{ATE.}\end{smallmatrix}$ *Rev. J. M. Durrell.*

Cancel "Great urbanity," etc., by writing in large letters, with different colored chalk, "Grace." Cancel "Fortunate circumstances," etc., with "Faith." The text then reads, "By grace are ye saved, through faith." Enlarge on faith. Heb. xi.

Blood Drops.

1. "Have mercy upon me, a sinner."	2. "Your sins and iniquities will I remember."	3. "A woman that was a sinner."
4. Taken in sin "in the very act."	5. "He was a thief in the past."	6. "How much evil he hath done."
7. Weary and heavy laden.	8. The host of Pharaoh— sin, misery, disobedience—pursue me.	9. Ragged in the far country.

These spots of scarlet and crimson must be canceled by blood drops from Calvary. Write over 1, "Justified;" over 2, "No more;" over 3, "Much forgiven;" over 4, "Go and sin no more;" over 5, "To-day with me;" over 6, "Peace with God;" over 7, "Rest;" over 8, "Under the blood;" over 9, "The best robe" Then, in large letters, below it all, "The past is all under the blood;" or, in place of 3, write, "Her sins which were many," and cancel it with "Forgiveness."

God Above All.

I AM OF $\begin{smallmatrix}\text{PAUL,}\\\text{APOLLOS,}\\\text{CEPHAS.}\end{smallmatrix}$

After describing the divisions and their cause (see Commentary) cancel the words "Paul, Apollos, Cephas," by

printing " God " in red over them, and then write above the
" I am " these words : " Be still, and know that," making the
sentence seen by the eye at the close, " Be still, and know
that I am God."

SATISFACTION.

" I SHALL BE
SATISFIED
WHEN I { AM HAVE

RICH,
FAMOUS,
POWERFUL,
AT REST,
A HOME,
A MILLION,
LEISURE,
SUCCESS.

Cancel " Am rich, famous, powerful, at rest," with " Awake
in his likeness." Cancel the four words after " Have " with
" Christ." Then write just beside " Satisfied " on the left,
" It," and on the right, " My longings as nothing else could
do," so that the prominent passages before the eye at the
close shall be, " I shall be satisfied when I have Christ, and
when I awake in his likeness," and also " It satisfied my longings as nothing else could do." Then, for the benefit of
the young, add at one side, " SATISFY US EARLY with thy
mercy, that we may REJOICE and be GLAD ALL OUR DAYS.

THE TRUE WORSHIP.

WORSHIP IN JERUSALEM. GERIZIM.

Cancel " Jerusalem " and Geriz'm " by writing over them,
in large letters, " Spirit ;" add " by " under " in ;" write
" God is a " over " Spirit," and you have Jesus' correction of
the woman at the well. The thoughts then presented are,
" God is a Spirit to be worshiped *in* the Spirit and *by* the help
of the Spirit." The evils of ritualism in all its forms may be
shown with this exercise.

11. THE ERASING EXERCISE.

Similar to the canceling exercise is the erasing exercise, in which the eraser is used to rub out one word, or passage sometimes, in order to substitute another.

LOVING JESUS.

George A. Peltz gives a very striking exercise of this class. At first on the board there is this sentence:

"WHY DO I LOVE JESUS?"

After talking a little of this to those who love Jesus he rubs out "Why," and "Do I love Jesus?" is his next point. Then he rubs out "Do" and the interrogation point, and "I love Jesus" stands before the school. Then "I" is rubbed out, and the exhortation "Love Jesus" remains. Then "Love" is erased, and "Jesus" is the only *word* the children see, which suggests the passage, "They saw no man save Jesus only."

HOW TO BE HAPPY THIS YEAR.

For New Year's Day the subjoined exercise may be employed. Print on the board—

A NEW YEAR.

Ask the children, "What was the first thing you said this morning?" ("A Happy New Year.") "What did you hear those words with?" ("Ear.") Rub out "Y." Then, "What do you do with the ear?" ("Hear.") Put on "H" before "ear." "Now how shall we make the new year a happy one? If we are not Christians what must we have to be happy?" ("A New Heart.") Add "T," and finish the talk with the words before the eyes of all—

"A NEW HEART."

This is given briefly, by memory, from "The Blackboard."

12. Word-Symbol Exercise.

This class includes all those exercises in which passages of Scripture or other words are shaped into symbols of Bible truth, as crosses, stars, plows, shields, ships, roads, etc. For example:

THE PRECIOUS CROSS.

H E

I S

PRECIOUS

BLOOD

PROMISES

FAITH

TO YOU

THAT

BELIEVE.

See 1 Pet. i, 11; 2 Pet. i. First and last, Christ is "precious" to all that believe. His "blood" is precious, and also the "promises" and "faith" by which we claim and apply it to our hearts. The whole forms the "precious" cross. It would be well to ask on the Sunday previous to the use of this that the scholars should find every thing that Peter calls "precious." Then write only "Precious" on the board before the school, getting the remainder from the scholars. The cross, as it is the most prominent symbol of our holy religion, is often formed in a way similar to that just indicated, in blackboard exercises, as the following examples will show:

Thou
shalt
call
HIS
"Believe on   name   and thou shalt
the LORD JESUS be SAVED."
for he
shall
save
HIS
people
from
their
SINS. *J. S. Ostrander.*

I love
them
that
love
"Come unto ME and be saved."
"My son, give ME thine heart."
& they
that
seek
ME
early
shall
find
ME. *Rev'd from I. W. C*

With this the passages may. be used : " Suffer the children to come unto me," etc. ; and also, " O satisfy us early with thy mercy, that we may rejoice and be glad all our days."

THE APOSTLE'S CROSS.

INFIRM-
ITIES,
DISTR-
ESSES,
PERSECUTIONS,
REPRO-
ACHES,
NECES-
SITIES,
FOR
CHRIST'S
SAKE.

The apostle says : " God forbid that I should glory save in the cross," and also, " I glory in infirmities,   . for Christ's sake."

THE EASTER CROSS.

HE IS
NOT
HERE.
EASTER MORNING.
HE IS
RISEN
AS HE
SAID.

MY LORD
AND MY GOD.

W. H. Sutton, of Jersey City, used an acrostic cross at a convention in that State.   He said : " I want to give you six reasons why Christ is the BEST FRIEND."

He illustrated this in the usual manner of blackboard representation—

The Best
F
R
I
E
N
D

He told appropriate stories to fill out these different capital letters. The first, expressing the conclusion that he was a *faithful* friend; the second, that he was our *Rescuer*, our *Redeemer ;* the third, our *Intercessor ;* the fourth, our *everlasting* friend; the fifth, he is always *near* us; the sixth, he *died* for us.

"Now, scholars, you can carry these conclusions in your mind. If I had not a blackboard I would take some other method: I might take my fingers, so that the illustration would come with a word on each finger. Dividing the subject in this way will help our scholars to carry home with them the thought that HE IS OUR BEST FRIEND."

THE LIFE OF CHRIST.

D Y I N G.
SUFFERING.
CLAIMING TO BE DIVINE.
SAVING A PUBLICAN.
TEACHING.
WORKING.
CLEANSING.
CONQUERING.
APPROVED.
QUESTIONED.
WELCOMED. *Rev. S. M'Gerald.*

This cross was used for a review of the life of Christ, but may also be used to illustrate the thought that not that dark Friday alone, but *the whole life of Christ, was a crucifixion.* At Bethlehem he nailed himself to the cross of a human life. Every tear shed over Jerusalem and at the grave of Lazarus was a drop of blood from one who was being crucified; every sigh and groan came from a heart pierced with a terrible spear.

The two expressions, " Christ's sufferings " and " Our salvation," may be made into a cross, the "S" being at the center for the second word in each.   A cross has also been made in connection with Joseph's life:

F^{OR}_{OR}

TEARS.
DROPS OF BLOOD.

J. H. Kellogg has given the following in connection with the offering of Isaac:

THOU   from ME. Genesis xii, 22.

Abraham offered his only son upon the mountain top		We should offer a broken and contrite
(Make sketch of mountain top and altar.)	F O R O U R S I N S. " They crucified him." Luke xxiii, 33.	
Gen. xxii, 12.		Psa. li, 17.

THE ANCHOR OF THE SOUL.

Our anchor: "If any man sin, we have an Advocate with the Father."   "This hope we have" attached "to the soul"

"as an anchor," by the cable of faith, "sure and steadfast."
"He that hath this hope in him purifieth himself."

Illustrations from incidents of sea-life will be appropriate,
and songs about sailing on the sea of life—"Clinging to the
Rock," "Land Ahead," "Homeward Bound," etc. In the
midst of a storm at sea, when the vessel was expected to go

down in a few moments, a sailor came up to a man who seemed very calm, and said, "Are you not afraid? the anchor has given way." "But," said the other, "I have an anchor to the soul, sure and steadfast."

The four word-symbol exercises following—The Christian Heart, The Shield of Faith, The Prize of Our High Calling, and The Key of Promise—are all by Rev. R. L. BRUCE, of Stoneham, Mass. They are so clear in their meaning that they hardly need any explanation, but will repay a careful study with many fruitful suggestions.

"LOVE IS THE FULFILLING OF THE LAW." Rom. XIII, 8–14.

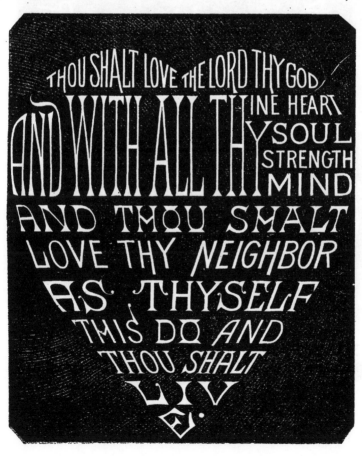

The Shield of Faith.

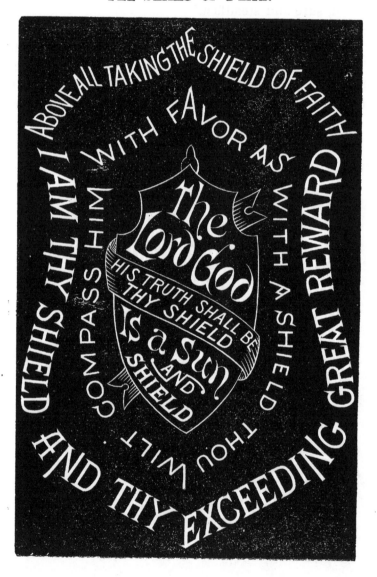

"LET NO MAN TAKE THY CROWN."

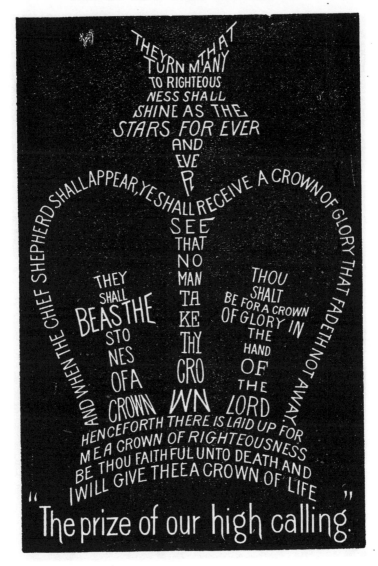

THE KEY OF PROMISE.

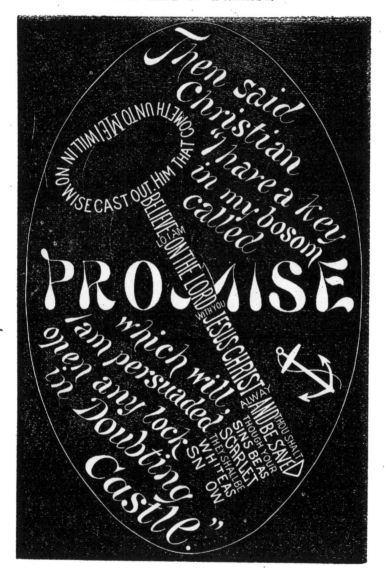

The Yoke of Christ.

COME UNTO ME ALL YE THAT LABOR AND ARE

HEAVY LADEN

I WILL GIVE REST TAKE MY YOKE UPON LEARN OF ME

IS EASY

"MY BURDEN

Is Light"

My Yoke is Easy. (Matt. xi, 30.)

I place first upon the board the two *U's*. I am about to address *you* and *you*, each of you. I want the ears and eyes of all. We are carrying *burdens*, guilt, sin, weighed down under the wrath of God. We are tired of sin, a burden; we are *heavy laden*. Jesus says, "Come unto me," etc. Will you come? He will tell *you* how to get rid of this load. He will teach *you*. He says, "*Learn of Me*." How? Why? *You* want *rest*. "*I will give you rest*." How? "Take *my* yoke upon *you*." How can we get rest by taking another yoke upon us? His yoke *is easy*. *We bear the yoke*. Christ bears our sins, etc. "Cast thy burden on the Lord," or Jesus, often. "Great peace have they that love thy law;" all joy, etc. Burdens light; "These light afflictions," etc. The invitation, "*Come unto ME all ye that labor and*," etc. The owner brings the yoke, and the oxen come under it. They assist in reaping the fields, and in winter live on the harvest, etc. Sometimes we see one ox lying down and the other standing, *both joined to one yoke*, one ready for work, the other at ease. So Christ waits for the idle Christian. "*Woe unto them that are at ease in Zion.*"—*J. S. Ostrander.*

THE MILESTONES OF THE NARROW WAY.

In the city of Rome distances were measured by milestones that counted in each direction from the golden milestone in the public square. So all along our way God puts up the milestones of the promises, beginning with the Golden Milestone of Conversion.

Make the outline of a road, with milestones, *each formed of the words of a promise.*

13. THE MAP EXERCISE.

This class includes simply geographical outlines and maps on the blackboard. Whenever the geography of a lesson is to be brought out, no means is more useful than a blackboard outline, on which the scholars can direct the blackboard de-

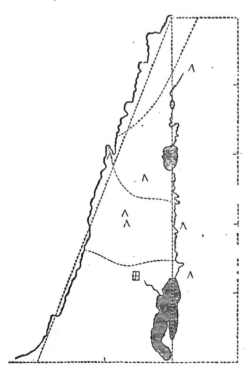

lineator in marking the prominent points.

A map whose construction the eye has witnessed will be retained more readily and vividly in the mind than one far more elaborate displayed when complete. The lack of exactness and finish will be more than compensated in the distinctness and impressiveness attained.

The outline here presented will be a convenient form of carrying the shape of Palestine in the memory.

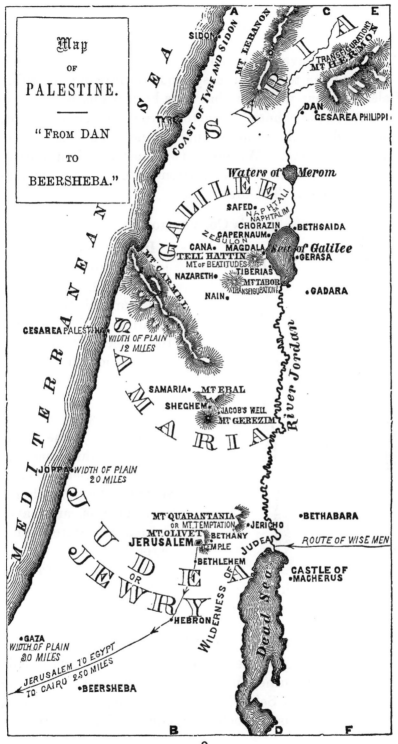

Map

OF

PALESTINE.

——

"FROM DAN

TO

BEERSHEBA."

SIDON

MT HERMON

SYRIA

TRANSFIGURATION?
MT HERMON

DAN
CESAREA PHILIPPI

COAST OF TYRE AND SIDON

TYRE

S E A

M E D I T E R R A N E A N   S E A

Waters of Merom

GALILEE

SAFED
NAPHTALI
NAPHTALIM
CHORAZIN
CAPERNAUM
ZEBULON
CANA
MAGDALA
TELL HATTIN
MT OF BEATITUDES
NAZARETH
NAIN

BETHSAIDA

Sea of Galilee
GERASA

TIBERIAS
MT TABOR
TRANSFIGURATION?

GADARA

MT CARMEL

CESAREA PALESTINA
WIDTH OF PLAIN
12 MILES

SAMARIA

River Jordan

SAMARIA
MT EBAL
SHECHEM
JACOB'S WELL
MT GEREZIM

JOPPA WIDTH OF PLAIN
20 MILES

MT QUARANTANIA
OR MT TEMPTATION
MT OLIVET
JERUSALEM
TEMPLE

BETHABARA

JERICHO

BETHANY

JUDEA

ROUTE OF WISE MEN

BETHLEHEM

JUDEA
OR
JEWRY

WILDERNESS OF

Dead Sea

CASTLE OF
MACHERUS

HEBRON

GAZA
WIDTH OF PLAIN
20 MILES

JERUSALEM TO EGYPT

TO CAIRO 250 MILES

BEERSHEBA

A   C   E

B   D   F

9

The plan we have just given and described is designed simply to afford the teacher an easy mode of drawing an outline of Palestine; but when one has thus been made, only one or two points in the country, those that are to be connected with the lesson, should be brought out, and no irrelevant parts of the map delineated. We insert two most excellent illustrations of this, which have been contributed to this book by Mrs. Samuel W. Clark. The first is on

SAUL'S CONVERSION.

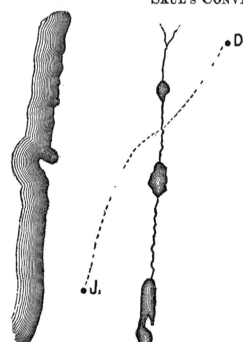

In connection with this journey from J. (Jerusalem) to D. (Damascus) the story of Saul's persecuting spirit, the light, the voice, the blindness with which he entered Damascus, and the other interesting incidents of his conversion, may be described. Some writer has said of this scene that "Christ himself stood as sentry for his little Church at Damascus, and saved it from its bitterest persecutor."

The following Sabbath the map was continued and enlarged to include a part of Paul's first missionary journey.

PAUL, THE FIRST MISSIONARY.

A careful reading of the Scripture narrative (Acts ix–xiii, 13) will give the journey indicated upon this map. A. is Antioch in Syria, S. is Seleucia, Sa. is Salamis, Ph. is Paphos, P. is Perga, A. P. is Antioch in Pisidia, and I. is Iconium.

A study of the history will enable the teacher to tell the story, not in stereotyped phrases, but as an interesting narrative of

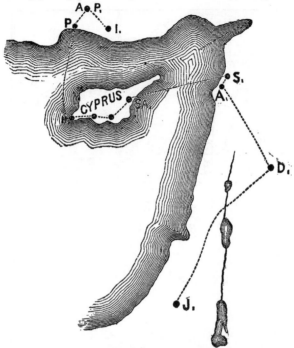

travel. As the history of Paul is continued on following Sabbaths, the new countries may be added and the three journeys kept distinct by three different colors of chalk. Only a little will be added to the map at once, and that thoroughly explained, so that at the close a life-long remembrance of Paul's wanderings will be secured. An interesting exercise may be conducted with this map, such as is suggested on pages 58, 59. The school may be divided into sections, *each of them having one of Paul's journeys*, on which they are to prepare. Then beginning with the map, as on page 130, the line may be increased and the places added, one after another, until all the journeys of Paul are completed, and he has "finished his course." Appropriate selections of Scripture, hymns, recitations, and readings will add to the interest of the exercise. The whole may be named, "From Damascus to Rome."

The following map will give a complete view of Paul's journeyings, as a basis for making these partial maps.

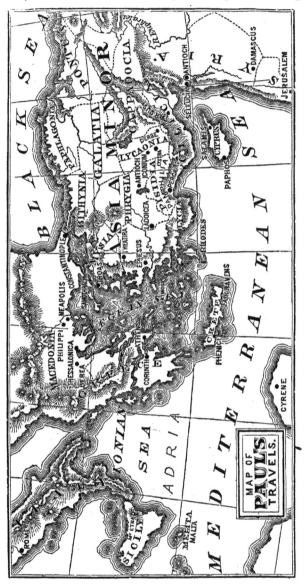

We give also, without special comment, the following specimens of this style of map drawing from the *Sunday-School Journal.*

FROM JERUSALEM TO BETHABARA.　THE SEA OF GALILEE.

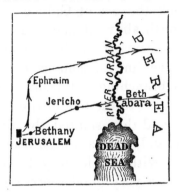 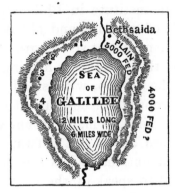

The two following diagrams will be a sort of square and dead level for making maps of parts or all of Palestine.

A MEMORY MAP OF　　TOPOGRAPHIC LINES OF
PALESTINE.　　　　　PALESTINE.

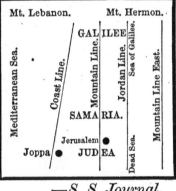

To make a memory map, (see diagram,) draw straight line A B perpendicular to C B, making C B nearly half as long as A B; join A C; divide A B into two equal parts at G, and G B into two equal parts at E; divide A C into three equal parts at F and D; join F G, and also D E. [1= Judea; 2=Samaria; 3=Galilee; D=Joppa; F=Mount Carmel. The Dead Sea commences a little below E, and the Sea of Galilee a little above G.] Surface diversified by mountains, rivers, plains, and ravines.—*Rev. J. Comper Gray.*

—*S. S. Journal.*

Dr. M'Cook, in a map which he made upon the blackboard at an institute in Philadelphia, took the Sea of Galilee as a unit of measure, and about one length above it placed Lake Merom; about six lengths below, measuring by the eye simply, the Dead Sea, making a crooked line to connect them, as the Jordan, with small streams branching out from it at appropriate places; about three lengths to the left of the Sea of Galilee he made Mount Carmel, and then slanted the line inward above and outward below, and, after a few additions of mountains and towns connected with the locality he desired to speak of, the map presented a very good representation of Palestine. If a variety of colors are used for water, shore, mountains, towns, rivers, etc., it will add greatly to the clearness and beauty of the map.

If the scholars can be induced to reproduce these maps from memory on their slates at home, and afterward bring them to their teachers, it will fix them yet more clearly in their mind.

Sometimes it is well to make a local map without the outline of the country as its frame-work, as the following for

CHRIST AT JACOB'S WELL.

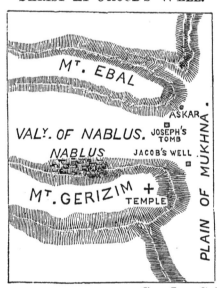

We add one more specimen of this class.

NAIN AND VICINITY.

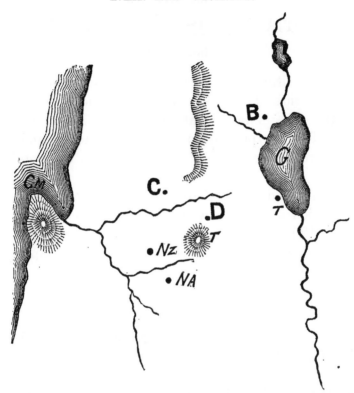

In telling the story of the miracle at Nain, this map may be used to show its position and the points of Bible interest that surround it. Cm. is Carmel, G. is the Sea of Galilee, B. is Bethsaida, Ti. is Tiberias, C. is Cana, Nz. is Nazareth, and Na. is Nain. Old Testament history connects many interesting events with this region.

SEED-THOUGHT.

The following may be made into a useful map by a rough sketch of the mountains and the sea, with tents in the midst, to show the perilous position of the Israelites.

THE SEA-PATH. (Exod. xiv, 9, 19–22, 27.)

MOUNTAIN.

EGYPTIANS.　　**ISRAEL.**　　SEA.

MOUNTAIN.

Describe the situation of Israel. The enemy behind, mountains on either side, the sea in front. But God opened a path through the sea. Israel went over. The Egyptians were drowned. The Egyptians trusted in their horses and chariots, Israel trusted in God. "*Some trust in chariots,*" etc. Psalm xx, 7.

Use the map not only historically, but also to show that when God bids us "go forward" he always clears our way as we go. "Though we pass through the waters, they shall not come nigh us." "Though a host should encamp against us, in God shall we be confident."

THE WANDERING PATH.

An excellent illustration of the going forward and backward, the faithfulness and faltering of many Christians, may be made by drawing the crooked line of the journey of the Israelites through the wilderness, marking not only prominent places, but also, at proper points, "Manna," "Brazen serpent," "Water from the rock," "Fowls from the heavens," to indicate God's goodness; and such passages as these, at other places, when they begin to turn back, "Much discouraged," "Longing for flesh-pots," "Rebelling," "Golden calf," etc., to represent not only the historical facts, but also our proneness to wander.*

* A concert exercise on this journey, entitled "The Christian Pilgrimage," has been prepared by the author of this book in connection with Dr. Eben Tourjée. The circulars are used both for concert and praise meetings, and are published by Eben Shute, 40 Winter-street, Boston, Mass. Price, $1 50 per hundred.

14. The Outline Exercise.

Last and best of all is the outline exercise—outline drawings for the illustration of truth.

Most of the outlines are only the putting into chalk of Bible metaphors and similes. Those of this kind are by far the best, and seldom is it well to represent any other outlines on a Sabbath-school blackboard. We might make one important exception in favor of the religious symbols of the Church, which are given at the close of this division. They offer a wide range for appropriate outline exercises. As a rule, elaborate outlines are a disadvantage, although a school that has an excellent artist may as properly have a beautiful picture on one side of its blackboard as on its wall. In almost every case the simplest outlines, drawn at the time of explanation without special effort at ornament or perfection, are the best.

From the Cradle to the Coffin.

Mr. Stout makes a very impressive lesson with a simple line:

C | ——————————————————— | C

He tells the schools that the line they see is the picture of every human life from the cradle to the coffin. Every one that hears him is at some point on that line. They all wish that point may be nearer the first " C " than the other, but it may be very near the last, etc. The same excellent speaker makes an impressive exercise for teachers by making two " Cs" as above, and then connecting them by a curve, saying, " The teacher's orbit should be from the closet of prayer to the class;" and then, making another curve from the second " C " back to the first, he adds, " and from the class to the closet."

Another very simple exercise comes to us from the ancients :

" Pythagoras used the letter Y as a symbol of human life. 'Remember,' says he, 'that the foot of the letter represents infancy, and the forked top the two paths of virtue and vice, one or the other of which people are to enter upon after attaining the age of discretion."

Another exercise as simple as that just mentioned is to represent with two lines, meeting at right angles, the coming together of

PHILIP AND THE EUNUCH.

After the story of their journeys and meeting is told, when the separation is mentioned, continue the lines so that they will form a cross.

The Treasurer of Candace found the cross as Philip "preached unto him Jesus" from the fifty-third of Isaiah. When the Christian is willing to obey the leadings of the Spirit, and the awakened one is desiring to know the way, God's providence will bring them together, and both shall be blessed. "Jesus in the Old Testament," "Drawing near to those we would benefit," "Preaching Jesus to single hearers by the roadside and fireside," and other such topics, may be presented from this story and outline.

THE FIRST LOVE LOST.

Another simple exercise is the accompanying star cross, that may be used with the letter to the Church at Ephesus in Rev. xi. There are seven stars, the angels of the seven Churches, and one of them is falling for lack of love. The Church at Ephesus had a grand record in some respects—works and labor and patience, indignation and punishment for evil-doers, endurance, and other virtues, but all was in vain for lack of love: "I have somewhat against thee because thou hast left thy first love." A similar failure is described in 1 Corinthians xiii.

THE CROSS.

The outline cross may be used with a variety of inscriptions. For example:

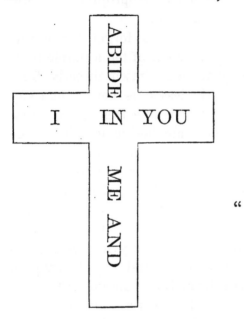

ASK WHAT YE WILL,

ABIDE
I IN YOU
ME AND

I WILL DO IT!

"

:

Words of Suffering.	Words of Love.
1. John xix, 28.	4. Luke xxiii, 34.
2. Matt. xxvii, 46.	5. Luke xxiii, 43.
3. John xix, 30.	6. John xix, 26, 27.
	7. Luke xxiii, 46.

1. Thirst.	4. Forgive.
2. Forsaken.	5. Paradise.
3. Finished.	6. Son, mother.
	7. Hand.

Or this:

Rebellion.

The ruin it wrought, and God's remedy. Num. xvi, 46–50.

Aaron   stood between   Jesus

"The Living."   "The Dead."

"Eternal Life."   "The Second Death."

1 Tim. ii, 5.

Or this, by T. B. Phipps:

THIS IS MY BELOVED SON.

JOSEPH,   JESUS,
Hated,   Rejected,
Envied,   Despised,
Enslaved,   Betrayed,
Imprisoned.   Crucified.
SUFFERED TO SAVE
His Brethren. | Me, a Sinner.
Conquered through Love, every
Knee shall Bow.

A. C. Chaplin, of Conway, Mass., gives the following excellent advice in regard to simple outlines to infant class teachers, but it may not be wholly inappropriate for others also:

"Do not forget that in nine cases out of ten a simple illustration, drawn directly from the lesson, is better than any other. If your lesson is on the 'Gadarene Demoniac,' draw an ancient tomb with a broken chain beside it. If on the 'Ten Virgins,' draw ten lamps, five burning and five gone out. If on death, natural or spiritual, draw two or three graves. If on 'Christ the Light of the World,' draw the rising sun shining upon a house with closed blinds. Such parables as 'The Builders,' 'The Friend at Midnight,' and some others, suggest their own pictures. A very interesting lesson may be made from the 'Mustard Seed' by drawing in colors a tree, full size (enlarge from Bible dictionary) of the mustard tree, and by its side a dot, representing the seed. An old-fashioned well on one side, on the other the name 'Jesus,' may furnish an introduction to a talk about the 'Living Water,' and so on indefinitely."

While we thus seek simplicity, distinctness must also be secured lest the exercise become ludicrous. A superintendent, having drawn what he intended for an *eye* on the blackboard, asked, "Now what do you see on the board?" A boy answered, "*an oyster shell.*"

Such answers will sometimes be given when the outline is correctly drawn, as the following illustration will show. Says J. S. Ostrander, "Not a great while ago I was present at a large Sunday-school meeting, in which one of our most successful teachers used the board to illustrate the idea of a sacrifice. He drew upon the board an altar, and upon it a lamb, around which he drew, with *red crayon*, representations of the consuming fire. The whole was well done. The children were pleased and instructed. 'What is this, children?' he said, pointing to the altar, lamb, etc., to all of which correct answers were obtained. Finally the simplicity and innocence of a little child was discovered by the putting of the following question by the speaker: 'And what is this?' (pointing to the *red chalk representation of fire*.) After some hesitancy a little voice out in the congregation responded, '*I guess they are the feathers of the lamb.*' Like a good questioner, the brother received the answer with respect, and proceeded to " simplify and repeat."

We will insert several simple and very impressive exercises on the life of Elijah, contributed by Mrs. Samuel W. Clark of Newark, as examples of simple outlines

Elijah Fed by Ravens.

A tree is rudely drawn, a line or two is made for ground, a perpendicular line beneath the tree represents the prophet, and four or five double curves represent the coming ravens in the familiar way in which children represent flying birds. These parts will be added, one after another, as they are described. This motto may be written above them, GOD SUP- PLIES OUR DAILY WANTS, and below

$$\text{ELIJAH} \begin{array}{c}\text{Loved}\\\text{Trusted}\\\text{Obeyed}\end{array} \text{GOD,}$$

I MUST DO SO.

The Poor Widow.

The story of the widow's poverty, and also of her bereave- ment, are represented by the rude outline of a gate in a wall of square stones, with the simple outline of a cottage just inside, and two perpendicular lines to represent the widow gathering sticks when she met the prophet. As the story is told the outline is made step by step, and on the board are the words,

GOD Cares for the Poor.
Helps in Sorrow.

THE ANSWER BY FIRE.

For the "answer by fire" on Carmel the outline of a mountain is drawn, with two altars, a fire blazing on one only. At its sides the trenches are represented by simple curves, and the prophet by a perpendicular line

THE ANSWER TO PRAYER

is represented by the sketch of a mountain top and a little cloud out over a simple representation of the sea, a perpendicular line representing the servant as he looks toward the cloud.

THE CAVE

where he heard the still small voice is represented by a dark spot looking like a cave on the side of another mountain.

[These exercises on Elijah are especially good for infant class use.]

JERUSALEM.

The simple outline of a place and its vicinity is easily made, and very helpful in geographical and historical study. We give on the following page an outline of Jerusalem, with the temple most prominently in view, as a specimen.

When the eastern plow, or the stones with which grinding was done, or the altar, or candlestick, or any other articles of household or temple use are mentioned, whose outlines are simple, they will be better understood than by any word description if a Bible dictionary is examined and the outline is sketched on the board.

I will briefly indicate how some of these simple outline exercises may be made for different themes without giving the cuts themselves.

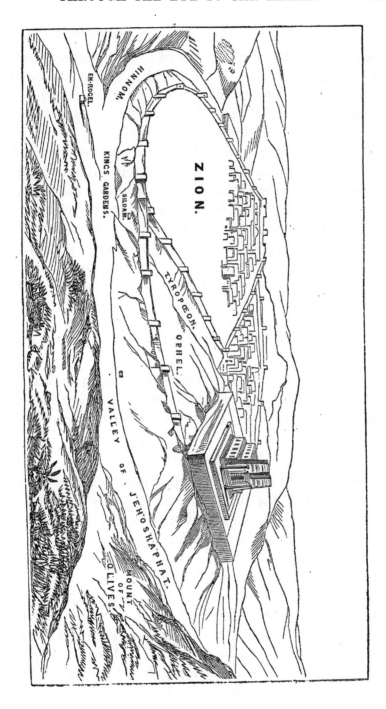

The Straight Road and its Monuments.

Draw a straight line on the board to represent an ideal life-journey. Speak of the actual life of most men as crooked, which might be represented by a crooked line, drawn to contrast with the straight one. The straight one is to represent the length of a life of threescore and ten years. Draw at the proper distance for ten years of age the representation of the *marble milestone : marble,* because of childhood purity, for this is the age when responsibility begins. Under it the Bible, as a guide in the straight road, to be taken up by the pilgrim-child as it passes this boundary. At the proper distance for twenty-five years of age represent the *silver milestone*: a clear, ringing life at this age, as solid and shining in virtue as silver. Beneath it represent a sword—the sword of the Spirit—which now must be wielded. At the proper distance on the line for sixty years of age, draw with yellow chalk the *golden milestone ;* under it a *pen :* golden because it is the harvest time. A pen there for writing the record of his life upon a scroll, which can be figured at the end of the line, to indicate that the life is finished and its record of good deeds left for others to read as they journey. Better than a gravestone.— *W. E. Huntington.*

The Two Paths.

The figure of life as a journey, just used, is one of the most frequent figures of the Bible. In many places it represents a right course of life in contrast with a wrong one, under the simile of two " ways," two " paths," etc.

Draw the simple outline of two roads branching out from a common corner, to the right and left. A little way below the left-hand path, at short intervals, put up the warnings found in Proverbs : " Avoid it ; " " Pass not by it ; " " Turn from it ; " " Pass away." Just at the entrance put the other warning, " Enter not." Along the left-hand road write, " The way of the wicked is as DARKNESS," (the word " darkness " at the end of the path.) By the side of the way put the

warning, "Go not," and also the words, "The end thereof,"
with a hand pointing to the end where are the words,
D_{eath."} "   On one side of the way write, "Bread of wickedness," "Wine of violence." Near the entrance of the right-
hand way write, {"Walk—Not faint." "Run—Not weary."   Through the midst of the
way write, "THE WAY OF THE JUST IS AS THE SHINING
LIGHT," ("light" being near the end of the way.) Beyond
it write, "PERFECT DAY." By the side of this path write,
"*Still waters*," "Green pastures," indicated by a few simple
lines and appropriate colors. Make a winding line leading
across the way, and mark it "Jabbok," as the wrestling-place of
prayer. Make also a lane across to "The Way of the Wicked,"
by which any can cross who will. On the other side make
a lane leading into "BY-PATH MEADOW" and "DOUBTING
CASTLE," (simply outlined.) Other parts of the Bible and
Pilgrim's Progress may also be used with this outline. At
the corner print "CHOOSE YE." Below the outline write—

WALK   THE   WAY.
OBEY   TRUTH.
LIVE   LIFE.

Along the left-hand path, to represent the gradual increase of
sinful habits, use the thoughts of the First Psalm: "Walketh
with unrighteous;" "Standeth with sinners·" "Sitteth with
scorners."

THE LOVE OF MONEY.

Tell the story of Gehazi's sin. Have the text repeated,
"*The love of money is the root of all evil.*"

Not money itself—we must have that and serve God with
it. Earn it; get it honestly; all you can, and use it for God.
Little children can do that. The love of it, coveting it, is the
evil root which produces only thorns. Did you ever see a
thorn-tree—every branch with great needle-points sticking
out in all directions? (If you can, show a large thorn or
branch of a thorn-tree.) Draw on the board a ragged root,
as if growing deep in the soil, write on its several parts,

10

"Love of money," "Root of evil." Above ground, make the branches sharp with thorns, writing on each branch as you question class, names of Gehazi's sins: "Coveting," "Lying," "Stealing," "Idolatry," "Profanity." (With colored crayon you can make a picture which, with forcible words, will make an enduring impression.) The verse says of money, "Some have coveted after and pierced themselves through with many sorrows." Did you ever get a splinter or thorn in your flesh? Suppose you did not tell mother lest she hurt you in taking it out, how it would fester and throb with pain! So the wounds of thorns from the evil tree of this wicked root. A Jewish soldier, Achan, once saw and coveted and stole a royal garment, some silver, and a wedge of gold. He buried them under his tent, but God brought it all out, and said that his tent and all that he had must be burned with fire, and he be stoned to death. A man and his wife once kept back part of the money they had promised to God. How their hearts were pierced by his hand, for at the very door where they lied to him they both fell dead!

Who betrayed Jesus Christ? For how much? How ought we to hate a sin that sold the dear Saviour. Are children ever tempted to covet, lie, or steal? Is it wrong to wish for a marble, a knife, a doll's dress or hat, hide it away and then keep it for our own? (Get remarks from the children upon such temptations.) Is it right to take a penny from papa's pocket, or a nickel from mamma's drawer? Are little sins as black in God's sight as big ones? Do people begin to sin by doing some terrible wrong? How do they learn? Years ago, in the State of Kentucky, a man was hung for highway robbery and murder. Before he was taken out of the jail a minister said, "How did you ever come to do such awful things?" "O," he said, "it was just as easy. I know the very hour I began. When I was a little boy a peddler came to our house and I stole a *paper of pins*, and my mother hid them for me; I went on stealing, and here I am." That wicked mother! If every stolen pin had been a spear, her heart could not have been more pierced with sorrows than it was by the wretched life and death of that son.

Where do all these wicked hearts go to at last? *Outside* that heaven we have learned so much about, shut out, will be all covetous, thieves, whosoever loveth and maketh a lie. How can we be kept safe from temptation and sin?—*Faith Latimer.*

The Heart Vineyard.

Draw heart, surrounded by hedge. Inside heart, a vine, etc. Ask what a vineyard is; what the vineyard is we each are to cultivate for God. Answer being given, write Vin. of Ht. Draw out of scholars what the Vine in our heart is; then what the fruits are. Ask what a hedge is. Used to keep out wild beasts; God surrounds our heart with hedge of Bible truth to preserve the vineyard from the devil, who goes about like a roaring lion, seeking, etc. Show that we must open the hedge ourselves before he can get in. Then wipe off lower end of heart to illustrate our giving admittance to the Adversary. Let the blackboard eraser represent the devil, who enters through the opening, erases the vine and fruits, and fills the heart with SIN, which write in large letters. Ask which the scholars wish to *have in their hearts, the* VINE *or the* DEVIL? See Isa. v, 4.—*Rev. J. M. Durell.*

A similar use of the outline heart was made in an address of Rev. A. H. Brown in New Jersey. He began by drawing a semi-heart-shaped line on the blackboard, and then said: By means of that chalk-mark I lay hold of the faculties of your minds. Adults though you may be, I have gained your attention, and you are penciling the thought upon the retina of the eye, which is soon to be transferred to the mind's retina. I have excited your curiosity. But what have we here? Mr. Chairman, if you will permit me I will take a little liberty this afternoon. I will imagine this audience is an audience of children. If I were at home I would ask my scholars or class some questions, but I will forego these questions to-day. We have here the outline of a heart marked on the blackboard—a mighty force-pump within us which is sending the bright-red current through our whole system even to the extremities: the hand, the face, are made beautifully red by this blood, even the hair is vivified by it. When I was a child I saw a little boy playing with his sister. They did not agree very well, and the little boy took a flat-iron and threw it at her. It laid her in death. What was it that caused that boy to throw the flat-iron? Was it the blood in the hand? Little Charlie was out playing. His poor, sick mother wanted him to come in. She called him, "Charlie, come in." "I won't." The mother, enfeebled by disease, shut the window and retired. After awhile, Charlie, tired with his playing, came in. He retired for the night. During the night his heart pained him. He thought of the word he told his mother, and said, "I will ask her to forgive me." In the morning he ran to the door of her chamber and knocked, but there was no answer. He went up to the bed and cried, "Mother! mother!" No answer. "Mother! mother! mother!" No answer. The white hand lay on the coverlet, and he took hold of it to waken his mother, but she was dead. His heart was wrung with agony as he cried, "O mother! mother! I am sorry that I said, 'I won't.'" What was it that made little Charlie tell his mother, "I won't?" Was it the blood in the lips? *No, it was sin, sin in the heart.* This "sin" I write with the charcoal. Why? Because it *soils.* SIN SOILS. You can never play with sin, children, without polluting yourselves. Remember that sin pollutes even if you touch it. Now, we have sin in the heart. We don't want it there, and how shall we get it out? You cannot rub it out. By attempting to do so you only make the matter worse. I turn to God's word—to the first Epistle of St. John—and I read, "The blood of Jesus Christ cleanseth from all sin." Let us write that there. I take a piece of red chalk, and write over the letters in the heart, "THE BLOOD OF JESUS." I cover the word SIN all up, and it takes it all away. It washes it all out. Nothing else can do it. "There is no other name under heaven given to men whereby they may be saved." Now, children, if you want to do right and not to do wrong, you have only to get Jesus in your heart first.

No Room for Christ. (Eccles. xii.)

Another heart outline may be made as follows: Draw a house, seemingly dilapidated and old. Above the house a few stars and the moon with many clouds. Then bring out the meaning of Solomon's allegory of the old man as a house and its surroundings:

"The keepers"—Hands.
"The strong men"—Legs.
"Grinders"—Teeth.
"Windows"—Eyes.
"Music"—Voice.
"Almond tree"—White hair.
"Desire"—Appetites.

Heart.

Around the house make the outline of a heart. To this house that God built for his own dwelling Jesus comes and knocks. Our hearts should be like the cottage at Bethany, always open to the Saviour. He comes and knocks. Shall we, like many, open to him and "sit at his feet," or, like the Church of Laodicea, let Jesus stand without and knock? Print "No Room for Jesus" across the picture, and after showing the ingratitude of such a course, erase "No" and leave it "Room for Jesus." Write also the motto within the heart outline: "Thy word have I hid in my heart, that I might not sin against thee."

The Heart Made Right.

We have compiled the following from an exercise of Dr. Vincent's and one by C. B. Stout:

H_OELP LESS.

Jesus meets a leper: "helpless," because his disease is beyond medicine; "hopeless," because there is little chance of recovery; "homeless," because even in sickness he is banished from his home, and none of his dear ones can administer to him. See, for further particulars, Bible Dictionary. Let a heavy straight line represent a leper. Jesus comes across him: intersect the first line so as to form a large white cross. Rub out "Less." Jesus' coming brings "Help, hope, home." The cross brings the same to us. Talk about the ancient shame of the cross, and how it became glorious. Then ascertain by questions that it is the symbol of Faith, and print an "F" on the board; then put a semicircle at the bottom, to make it into an anchor, and ask the children what is thrown out in times of danger to hold the vessel; ascertain that the anchor is the symbol of Hope, and print an "H" below the F; then from the top of the cross carry lines in both directions to the hooks of the anchor, making a heart which includes an anchor and a cross. The heart is the symbol of Love. Write "L;" then show that Love means Charity, and you have "F, H, L"—Faith, Hope and Charity, and as the heart is greater than the cross or anchor, so the greatest of these three qualities of heart is Charity, which includes both the others: "It *hopeth* all things, *believeth* all things." Instead of a heart "Helpless, homeless, hopeless," and cursed with the leprosy of sin, we have now a heart with Faith, Hope, and Love filling it. Illustrate each step in the exercise.*

The Book of Life.

The "Book of Life" has been used in a great variety of blackboard exercises, the book being usually drawn on the board with two pages in sight. (A large blank book with some of the pages blotted, some of them neatly written, and most of them pure white, to represent the future, may well be

---

* Almost every religious subject has some excellent illustrations in "Foster's Cyclopedia of Illustrations."

used with this subject. If it be New Year's, let the whole book be free from writing, with spotless pages.) On the book write " Book of Remembrance," or " Book of Life." Read Luke x, 17–24. Now what shall the angels write on each day's page? Let us see. Now let us take one page. What were John's first thoughts when he waked? What did he first do? (And so on; setting down on the blackboard such acts as seem natural for the class addressed. Some sin, not so gross as stealing, may be more appropriate. Let this depend upon the state of the class.)

> **FIRST DAY.**
>
> John wakes up; calls to mind Jesus' love.
> John rises from bed.
> John prays to Jesus.
> John obeys and helps his mother.
> John goes to school and studies well.
> John, coming home, sees some nice apples.
> John takes the apples.
> John confesses his sin to Jesus.

When the prayer of confession to God is offered, and fully explained, then rub out the sin he committed. If we confess our sins, God is just and faithful (keeps faith) to forgive us our sins.

Draw a page for the second day, and send John back to the store to return the stolen apples, or otherwise make confession and restitution to the owner.

> **SECOND DAY.**
>
> John prayed.
> John took back the stolen apples.

I remember, years ago, when I was a school-boy, the teacher used to keep a little book with the name of each scholar in it, and a record of how we behaved, learned our lessons, etc. We received tickets according as we did well in these two things. At the end of the term she looked over this little book, and the one who had received the largest number of tickets, and therefore had been the best behaved and most studious scholar, was presented with a prize. It depended upon what was down on the little book against our names which one should receive the prize.

I once went into a court-room. It was the last day of the trial of a man for stealing. The lawyer was reading from sheets of paper what different persons had said about the criminal and his crime. What was written on these sheets of paper they called the *evidence*. The jury were listening to this evidence, and it depended upon what it was whether the criminal should be punished or not. Now let me take the Bible and read something that is very much like what I have been telling you about. Rev. xx, 11–13. Inforce these points: 1. God keeps account of all we do. 2. We are to be judged, at the end of the world, according to this account. 3. JESUS ONLY can take away the sins written against us in God's record.

Seed-Thought and Illustrations for this Subject

Ambition of men to make their names famous; to have their names among the lists of the brave, the learned, the honorable. Great sacrifices to secure this. How few names survive. Earthly fame perishable; names and lists both soon forgotten. But there is one imperishable record—the Book of Life. Names written there are not for time, but for eternity. A royal list of the King's friends. Ahasuerus, and the record of his reign. Names and deeds forgotten there; but the Book of Life is a Book of Remembrance. How blessed the thought that Jesus knows his lambs by *name*. Not one shall be left out. None *but* his saints entered there. False estimate often made here, and names of unworthy entered. There, every unworthy name blotted out. "To him that overcometh."

It is impossible for us to atone, or settle, the record of sins that God has against us. He knew this; and he "so loved the world—us—that he gave his only begotten Son," that by the shedding of his blood the great debt of sin might be paid. And Jesus permits us to *use his name*, so that if we come to God, humbly repenting our sins, and pleading the merit, sacrifice, and *name* of our Saviour, "*for his name's sake*" we may be forgiven, and the great debt of our sins be wiped out. The third thing to remember, then, is, " *Jesus only* can take away the sins written against us in God's record." He alone can pay the debt for us. Pause for a moment and sing with me, " Jesus paid it all."

And now let me tell you what idea a little mission Sunday-school boy in New York had about these great Record Books. He had learned to love Jesus at the Sunday-school. He was taken violently ill with inflammatory rheumatism, and though the pain was sometimes so severe that he was bent nearly double with it, yet he bore all patiently, speaking often of the worse pain Jesus had. borne for him. At last the doctor had to tell him that he could not live, and at the end of a terrible pain he exclaimed, " Good pain! good pain! that takes me to Jesus." The good lady with whom he lived stood by, weeping to see him suffer so, and asked him if he was sure he should go and see Jesus.

" O yes," said he ; " I shall be put in the ground a little while, and then God will come riding on a big cloud, and he will call, ' John Dean, stand up!' and I shall come out of my grave, and stand up there before him : then he will take a big book, and turn over leaf after leaf till he comes to my page—every body has a page, and every time they sin God puts it down —but when he comes to my page he wont find any thing."

"Why, John," said the lady, " have you never sinned ? "

" O yes ; but Jesus went, a good while ago, and took the book out of God's hand—found my page, and then, opening a little hole in his hand, let the crimson drops run on the book, and with the other hand wiped them all down the page, so when God looks he will see nothing but Jesus' blood. Then he will say, ' John, you go over there among the angels.' "

These directions and illustrations are compiled from three exercises in "The Blackboard " for May, 1871, one of them by D. B. Hixon, another by Horace B. Smith, and the third by the editor. The familiar tract of the American Tract Society, " How it was Blotted Out," is a very excellent illustration for this subject. Also the following: An officer in one of our hospitals was very sick, and not expected to live. One of the nurses in going her rounds heard a voice say "Here." Supposing it a call for her, she went to several beds, and at length to the officer, and said, "Did you speak?" He opened his eyes with a smile of joy and said, "O I thought I was in heaven, and they were calling the roll, and when it came to my name I said Here." If we would say "Here" in heaven we must also say "Here" to such "heavenly visions" as Paul's, which show what we must "do" and "suffer."

The Scroll.

Write on a scroll the words spoken at the Jordan, "This is my beloved Son, in whom I am well pleased." The baptism at the Jordan was properly the inauguration of Christ's ministry. Earth greets him with the cry, "Behold the Lamb!" Heaven echoes, "This is my beloved Son." Thus God gave Christ his credentials, while the Father's voice and the Spirit's presence centered around the other person of the Trinity, then "in the form of a servant."

The Eastern scroll can be used in a great variety of ways on the blackboard to inscribe Bible promises, messages, titles, etc. Almost every passage beginning "Thus saith the Lord," could be thus used. The commission and promise of the ascension, "Go ye into all the world," etc.; the commission to Peter, "Feed my lambs," etc.; also in John xiv, 23, 27, or any of the messages sent from one to another in the Bible— all such as these may well be put on a scroll, and thus made more impressive.

The Scroll of Wisdom.

The following is another specimen. Make an opened scroll held by two hands. Across the right hand print "Length of Days;" across the left, "Wisdom and Honor." On the middle of the scroll, "Happy is the man that findeth Wisdom."

Our Rock.

Make the simple outline of a rock and above it write, "*He brought honey out of the* Rock." (The last word should be on the rock.) Or use some other of the many passages about "the Rock" that represent Christ. Illustrate, after explaining the symbol, (perhaps using a fragment of rock as an object-lesson with the outline,) with the following incidents:

The Rock Fountain.—I was staying at a poor village near the sea-coast where the people had to bring all their water from a well. At all hours of the day little feet and great might be seen passing along a narrow lane, with every kind of pitcher, kettle, and can, to the well.

"Is this well ever dry?" I inquired.

"Dry? Yes, ma'am; very often in hot weather."

"And if it dries up?"

"Why, then we go to the spring higher up—the best water of all."

"But if the spring higher up fails?"

"Why, ma'am, that spring never dries up—never. It is always the same, summer and winter.

I went to see this precious fountain which "never dries up." The water was clear and sparkling, running down the high hill with the steady flow and soft murmur of fullness and freedom. It flowed down to the wayside, and was within reach of every child's little pitcher. The thirsty beast of burden knew the way to the spring that "never dries up."

Thank God for the good gift of water. He who gave the Jews "honey out of the rock and oil out of the flinty rock" gives us the rock fountains of water on every hand. Under the ruby of the wine is hidden passion, crime, and death; in the sparkle of water there is health, wealth, and purity. Happy is the man whose physical strength is founded on the Rock Fountain, whose political principles are built on Plymouth Rock, and whose faith has laid for its corner-stone the "Rock of Ages."

HIGH UP ON THE ROCK.—Once upon a time there lived a powerful king, who reigned over a large and fertile country. He had crowns of gold and pearls, and scepters of ivory and precious stones. His treasury was full of the costly things of the earth; tens of thousands of armed men were ready to obey his bidding, and his dominion extended from sea to sea. But without God's blessing worldly possessions are but an increase of care, and as this mighty monarch feared not God he was ever dissatisfied and unhappy.

In the dominions of the king there lived a certain dervise, famed for abstinence, sanctity, wisdom, and piety ; and the king, willing to profit by the instructions of the holy man, paid him a visit. He found him in sackcloth, living in a cave surrounded with high rocks on the borders of a wilderness.

"Holy man," said the king, "I come to learn how I may be happy."

Without giving any reply, the dervise led the king through the rugged pathways of the place till he brought him in front of a high rock, near the top of which the eagle had built her aerie.

"Why has the eagle builded her nest yonder ? "

"Doubtless," replied the king, " that it may be out of the way of danger."

"Then imitate the bird," said the dervise : " build thy throne in heaven, and thou shalt reign there unmolested and in peace."

Now the king would have willingly given the dervise a hundred pieces of gold, if he would have accepted it, for this precious piece of advice. It may be as useful to you as to the king, for you are all as much interested in being happy as he was. As the eagle built her nest on the rugged rock, build your hope on the " Rock of Ages." As the dervise told the king to erect his throne in heaven, so I tell you to " seek those things which are above, where Christ sitteth on the right hand of God. Set your affections on things above, not on the things of the earth." Do this, and you will be above the reach of danger for time and eternity.

The Cup of Blessing. (Psa. xxiii, 5.)

Draw outline of a cup upon the board. Question the pupils as to the various blessings received from God, and as the names are given write them on the cup, as, "Sunday-school, food, clothes, home, friends, Bible," etc. It is better, perhaps, to put only the initials of these answers on the cup. The "Sunday-school," written at the top, will cause the cup to overflow. Describe each soul as holding out a cup toward our heavenly Father, who daily fills it with mercies of inestimable value. The obvious lesson of heartfelt gratitude will, of course, be earnestly impressed by the teacher.—*James H. Kellogg.*

The Glory of Jesus.

Print the word " Jesus " in large white letters. Represent *glory* with radiating lines of yellow, diverging in every direction. Amid these lines print " Redemption," " Victory," " Rest," " Praise," " Holy Companionship," " Endless Joy," " Forever."—*Selected.*

'Tis Buts.

Draw a square box such as Sunday-school classes often use to keep their money in. Label it " 'Tis buts," and the following selected remarks will suggest what may be said about it.

" *'Tis but* five minutes past time for school-call; I'm not very late," says the tardy school-boy. Yet it is an offense that, oft repeated, brings disgrace to that boy and a black record on his school report.

" *'Tis but* a few cents a day I spend for my cigars or tobacco," says the youth just merging upon manhood, who thinks that in order to be manly he must adopt the filthy habits of man. If this youth would take his pencil and figure up the amount of his *'tis buts* spent in this way for one year, then for ten years, we think he would surprise even himself.

"'*Tis but* a dime or two a day I spend for my ale or beer," says the "*occasional*" tippler. If he will take time to estimate the amount of these '*tis buts* for a few years, as they would appear on his bank book, if deposited in a savings bank instead of down his throat, we think he will see the truth of that old English proverb, "*Pennies make pounds*," or, "Take care of the pence, and the pounds will take care of themselves."

Take care of your '*tis buts*—in time, in money, in all things.

THE SHIELD OF FAITH.

On a shield drawn on the blackboard place the following:

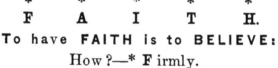

> * * * * *
> **F   A   I   T   H.**
> To have **FAITH** is to **BELIEVE:**
> How ?—* **F** irmly.
> When ?—* **A** lways.
> In what ? { * **I** n God and
>   * **T** he Bible,
>   * **H** is holy word.

Illustrate especially the need of *firm, unchanging* belief in God and the Scriptures.—*Jas. H. Kellogg.*

OVERCOMING.

The passages in Revelation beginning "Him that overcometh" may be grouped on a shield, three words being on a sword above it ("That" being on the guard and "Him—overcometh" on the handle and blade) and the remainder of each passage on the shield.

CREDO.

It is said that an old knight had as the device and motto of his shield an open Bible and the word "Credo"—*I believe*—below it. Make a shield with this device and motto, and by its side an acrostic, thus:

I BELIEVE IN

C hrist.
R edemption.
E verlasting Life.
D uty.
O vercoming through Christ.

THE CROWN OF LIFE.

Make an outline crown with the word "LIFE" upon it, the rays diverging from it downward shining through the words "Tribulation," "Persecution," "Distress." Underneath, a sword, on the hilt of which is written "*Be ;*" on the blade, "*thou faithful ;*" on the guard, "*unto death.*"—*Selected.*

THE LIGHT-HOUSE.

A light-house in simple outline, with the upper light representing Christ and the lower lights his people, can be used for many passages and teachings of the Bible, especially, "I am the Light of the world," and "Ye are the light of the world." A vessel or two in the distance, and a few clouds, will improve the same. For illustrations see Foster's Encyclopedia, 3026, 3027, 3040.—*Selected.*

THE STAR IN THE EAST.

George A. Peltz makes an impressive exercise by drawing a star with rays diverging across the blackboard, and below it the following:

JESUS { RIVERS—DESERTS / DANGERS — TOILS / SELF-DENIAL / CROSS-BEARING | PERSIA. / SIN

The star is above the word "Jesus," and the slanting rays fall through "Persia" and "Sin."

THE BOW OF CONSPIRACY. (Dan. vi, 4–10.)

Draw the outline of a bow on the board with the word "CONSPIRACY" scattered letter by letter around the curve of the bow. The arrow ready to fly—on its head, "Jealousy." Along the arrow "Darius's Decree," the feathered end marked "Hate." One side of the string marked "Presidents, Princes;" the other side "Counselors, Captains." Opposite the bow draw a shield, marked, "His truth shall be thy shield." Against this, afterward, a broken arrow may be represented, and the bow may also be erased and a broken one take its place. Scripture references: "Above all taking the shield of faith." Eph. vi, 16. "The wicked have drawn out the sword, and have *bent their bow*," etc. Psa. xxxvii, 14.

The Gospel Ship.

Draw an outline of a ship. Mark its sails "Faith," its lower edge "Works, ballast," its working rigging "Prayer," its prow "Perseverance," which is cutting through waves marked "World," "Flesh," "Devil;" the rudder is marked "Love of Christ," and the bands that unite it to the ship, "Nothing shall separate us." The flag at the stern is a red cross on a white field, the halyards marked, "I am not ashamed of the Gospel of Christ." At the masthead is a signal flag (suggested by Nelson's) with the inscription, "God expects every man to do his duty." On the stern of the vessel are the name and place of building: "Gospel Ship—Heaven." The anchor is formed of a text thus divided: Cross bar, "If any man sin—;" upright, "We have an Advocate with—·" claws, "The Father." This exercise is taken mostly from a sermon of Rev. T. De Witt Talmage.

The Promises—Our Mountain Tops.

Taking Bible geographies or Bible dictionaries to get the general outline and shape of the following mountains, draw them and connect them together, as if a group, with the inscriptions indicated written upon them. Sinai—"Draw nigh unto God, and he will draw nigh unto you." (Incident of Moses.) Moriah—"God will provide." (Isaac.) Horeb—"Thou wilt keep him in perfect peace whose mind is stayed on thee." (The "still, small voice.") Carmel—"Whatsoever ye shall ask in my name I will do it." (The little cloud.) Zion—"They that trust in the Lord shall be as Mount Zion that cannot be removed, but abideth forever." Nebo—"There remaineth therefore a rest to the people of God." (Moses' view of Canaan.) Olivet—"Him that cometh to me I will in nowise cast out." (The woman that was a sinner and had "much forgiven" at Bethany.) So these promises lift us above the dead level of earth "quite to the verge of heaven."

The following extract from one of the sermons of T. De Witt Talmage may be used to illustrate this exercise:

If a man has become a Christian, the thunders of Sinai do not frighten him. You have, on some August day, seen two thunder-showers meet. One cloud from this mountain, and another from that mountain, coming nearer and nearer together, and responding to each other, crash to crash, thunder to thunder, boom! boom! And then the clouds break and the torrents pour, and they are emptied, perhaps into the very same stream that comes down so red at your feet that it seems as if the carnage of the storm-battle has been emptied into it. So in this Bible I see two storms gather, one above Sinai, the other above Calvary, and they respond one to the other—flash to flash, thunder to thunder, boom! boom! Sinai thunders, " The soul that sinneth, it shall die;" Calvary responds, "Save them from going down into the pit, for I have found a ransom." Sinai says, " Woe! woe!" Calvary answers, "Mercy! mercy!" and then the clouds burst, and empty their treasures into one torrent, and it comes flowing to our feet, red with the carnage of our Lord—in which, if thy soul be plunged, it shall go forth FREE—FREE.

THE ALTAR OF THE UNKNOWN GOD.

Make the simple outlines of two altars. Over one print " ATHENIAN'S ALTAR," over the other " PAUL'S ALTAR." On the first inscribe "To the Unknown God;" on the other, " To God that made the world, and all things therein." There are many passages in Hebrews where an outline altar might be used.—*Selected.*

The Gospel Trumpet.

Make the outline of a trumpet and inscribe on it, "Go ye into all the world and preach the Gospel to every creature." On the flag that hangs from it, "The blood of Jesus Christ cleanseth from all sin."—*R. L. B.*

Looking Back from the Plow.

Draw the outline of an Eastern plow, and, by the help of a Bible dictionary, ascertain its peculiarities. After explaining these write upon it, "No man having put his hand to the plow and looking back is fit for the kingdom of God." Show that the Christian life means *work;* it must be our *great work.* Show how the sins of Eve, Cain, Gehazi, Lot's wife, and others, began with a *look* toward sin. As Cincinnatus was called from the plow to be Dictator, so we are taken from the plow to be kings in glory.

The Christian's Rosary.

Draw a string of beads large enough for a word or two on each bead. (A real rosary, Roman Catholic or Pagan, used as an object-lesson, will add to the interest of this exercise.) Write a name of Christ on each bead, "Jesus" being largest and most central. Go through the list, (not more than a dozen, and these the most familiar names of Jesus being taken, the children themselves telling you a name for each bead,) telling the meaning and especial blessedness or appropriateness of each of Christ's names, closing with "Jesus." After each name is mentioned a familiar verse which contains that name may be sung.

The Temple of Christian Character.

Represent a house or temple built of large square stones, on each of which one of the qualities of Christian character mentioned in Rom. xii may be written or indicated. On the foundation stone " Love," (v. 9;) on another stone " Abhor evil ; " another, " Cleave to good ; " and so on until the cap-stone is " Overcome evil with good."

The Prodigal.

Draw a large isosceles triangle, one point representing, with a sort of marsh about it, the " far country." The opposite line represents his home, the two lines that intersect at the far country being the roads by which the far country is reached. To get back he goes directly across from the far country to his home by means of a suspension bridge marked " Blood of Christ." He was " far off by wicked works," with a chasm between him and the Father ; he is " brought nigh " by Christ making his suffering body a bridge over the chasm. A house was burning, and a man made his body a bridge from one of its windows to the window of the next house, and although in great peril and pain, allowed all who were in the burning house to pass over to the other.

Redeeming the Time.

An admirable exercise for Watch Night or New Year's is furnished by Rev. R. L. Bruce, who draws a metaphorical clock with the usual face and a winged hour-glass above it. Over the clock is written the passage, " Behold, now is the accepted time ; " below it, " There shall be time no longer." On the frame-work of the clock opposite the numeral I, " Ye know not when the time is ; " near III and IV, " Watch and pray ; " near VI and VII, " At evening time it shall be light ;" near VIII and IX, " The time is now far past ; " near XI and XII, " The time is short." Then on the narrow rim of the dial, just outside the numerals, this passage : " The time cometh when I shall no more speak unto you in parables, but I shall show you the Father plainly." On the outer edge of the alarm dial, " It is high time to awake out of sleep ; " on the short hand, " How short my time is ; " on the long hand, " It is time to seek the Lord."

ILLUSTRATIONS

We give below two blackboard exercises that may be used to illustrate the simple use of blackboard outlines, at the same time affording seed-thought for addresses on *the teacher's most important work* and *the mission of the Bible in the Sunday-school.*

THE CONVERSION OF CHILDREN.

This is the great object of the Sunday-school teacher. So long as this is not gained, so long he must confess that he has failed of his mark.

Draw the outline of a target, the center spot white, the first ring red, the next blue, the next black. The following extract, clipped from an address of Rev. Dr. W. M. Taylor, of New York; will show the application to be made:

In a target there is a white center, surrounded by concentric rings of various colors—red, blue, and black. The archer, standing at a distance, takes his aim. If he hits the black ring—well, it is not a very bad shot, but it is not a success, either. If he hits the red one, that is not a success; he is not satisfied until he hits the target in the white center. Just so in teaching the child, you have a central aim with concentric rings. One may be his understanding of the words of the lesson; another may be his understanding of the location of the places and the manners and customs of the peoples; but, at the same time, there is the white center, the conversion of the soul, and until we hit the target there we have failed as teachers.

THE BIBLE TO ENLIGHTEN AND SAVE.

Draw in outline the pulpit or desk of the Sunday-school, surrounding it by waves, as if it were a light-house; then draw the Bible at the top with rays of light shining from it, as if it were the lamp. Write below the motto of the light-house on the coast of Cornwall, "To GIVE LIGHT, TO SAVE LIFE," and show that the use of the Bible in Sunday-school is not only to *teach*, but also to *save* the scholars. (Psa. xix, 7.) Other analogies to the light-house will be naturally suggested.

The Day Star.

Under this title we give an exercise by Rev. T. B. Appleget, somewhat modified from the original:

In a recent talk to a Sunday-school I gave an account of a party who sailed to the Southern Ocean, where they remained some time; told of their anxiety to get home, and of their joy when on their homeward trip their lookout reported the "Polar Star" in sight, etc. I explained the geographical position by a drawing on the board, thus— 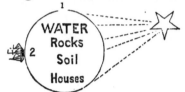 Showing how when they were at (1) they could see the star, but that at (2) they could not, on account of the *earth*, or *world*, which was composed of dense *matter*, such as *rocks*, *soil*, *water;* these I wrote in the circle. I then called attention to *Jesus* as the "Day Star," and showed how "the world," by which we meant *self*, *dress*, *wealth*, *pleasure*, *business*, etc., would get between us and *Jesus*, so that we could not see him. At this time the board looks like this:

Then I explained how we could *subject* these things—*come over* or "*overcome the world*," so that it should not interfere with our religion, and altered the illustration, as here: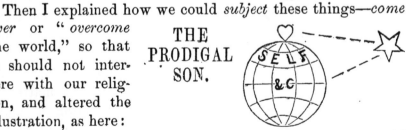

Two young men, one in rags, the other in purple, one amid husks, the other "faring sumptuously," *both felt the need of Christ's light in their hearts.* "Self, pleasure, wealth," were between the rich young man and Christ; the prodigal put all of self under his feet, and the light of mercy and love shone upon his heart.

God Loved the World.

J. C. Proctor has an exercise in which he represents the world resting on a block marked " Love " and that block on a threefold block marked " God " and that on nothing. The outline of a hemisphere may be roughly drawn in the circle, representing the earth and this passage arranged about it :

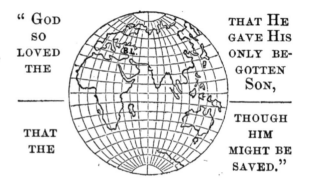

" GOD SO LOVED THE

THAT HE GAVE HIS ONLY BE-GOTTEN SON,

THAT THE

THOUGH HIM MIGHT BE SAVED."

" JESUS ONLY."

This exercise we have revised from one given by Rev. C. W. Barnes ·

"Thinking upon this, I went by a blacksmith's shop, and in a wheel, leaning against a post, I saw a good illustration.

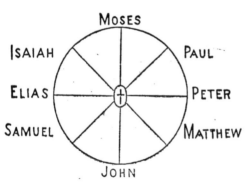

1. No matter how well the spokes might be fastened in the felloe, they needed to be morticed into the hub, every one. So all the books of the Bible are supported by Jesus. 2. No matter in what direction a spoke came from, there ·was a place in the hub for it. So every book testifies of Christ. 3. As the spokes approach the hub they get nearer together until they are lost sight of in the hub. So as the books come to talk of Jesus, they become *all one in Christ Jesus.*"

Not only may this exercise be used to represent the unity of the Bible in the cross, but also the unity of the Churches, by writing the names of Luther, Calvin, Wesley, Bunyan, Hooker, and three familiar names of evangelical preachers in the vicinity, in place of the Bible names above, and then showing how they all unite around the cross.

THE TWO LADDERS.

And he dreamed, and behold a ladder set upon the earth, and the top of it reached to heaven: and behold the angels of God ascending and descending on it.—GEN. xxviii, 12.

Her feet go down to death; her steps take hold on hell.—PROV. v, 5; MATT. vii, 13; ISA. v. 14; PSA. ix, 17; LUKE xvi, 24; MATT. x, 28.

The Heavenly Ladder.

The Ladder to Hell.

	The Heavenly Ladder		The Ladder to Hell
Last ☞ Step.	**Glory.** Matt. xxv, 34; Psa. lxxiii, 24.	First ☞ Step.	**Disobedience.** Rom. i, 30; Titus i, 16.
	Self-Denial. Luke ix, 23; Titus ii, 12, 13.		**Lying.** Rev. xxi, 8; John viii, 44.
	Usefulness. Eccles. ix, 10; 1 Cor. xv, 58.		**Sabbath-Breaking.** Ezek. xxii, 8; xx, 13.
	Obedience. 2 Cor. x, 5; Isa. i, 19.		**Swearing.** Lev. xix, 3; Zech. v. 3.
	Joy. John xvi, 22; Psa. xvi, 11.		**Stealing.** Lev. xix, 11; 1 Cor. vi, 10.
	Hope. Rom. viii, 24, 25; 1 Pet. i, 13.		**Gambling.** Luke xii, 15; 1 Tim. vi, 9, 10.
	Love. John xiv, 23; 1 John iv, 16–18.		**Drinking.** Isa. v, 11; Prov. xxiii, 31, 32.
	Peace. Isa. xxvi, 3; John xiv, 27.		**Murder.** Gen. ix, 6; Gal. v, 21.
	Faith. Rom. x, 17; Eph. vi, 16.		**Despair.** Prov. xi, 7; Job xi, 20.
First ☞ Step.	**Repentance.** Luke xiii, 3; 2 Pet. iii, 9.	Last ☞ Step.	**Destruction.** 2 Thess. i, 8, 9; Matt. xxv, 41.

Left side margins: 2 COR. v, 17. — CHRIST. — ROM. viii, 35–39.
Center: PSA. ciii, 8–11. — REV. xx, 10. — MERCY. — EXOD. xxxiv, 6, 7. — SATAN. — 1 PET. v, 8.
Right side margins: ROM. vi, 23. — SIN. — 1 PET. iv, 18.

Read DEUT. xxx, 19.

—*Selected.*

The Ladder to Heaven.

The ladder of Jacob's vision may also be represented, each of its rounds labeled with one of the virtues: Faith, Virtue, Knowledge, Temperance, Patience, Brotherly Kindness, Charity; or with one of the fruits of the Spirit: Love, Joy, Peace, Meekness, Gentleness, Patience, etc. By these we climb to heaven.

> " Heaven is not reached by a single bound,
>   But we build the ladder by which we rise
> From the lowly earth to the vaulted skies,
>   And we mount to the summit round by round.

Or the prominent events of Christ's life may be written on the rounds, for it is by them that we climb up to God. Write, "Manger," "Carpenter's Shop," "Asleep," "Weary," "Gethsemane," "Pilate's Hall," and on the highest round "Calvary." Jesus cries, "It is finished!"—the Jacob's ladder of the race, that shall enable them to reach heaven, is "finished." The top round should be in the shape of a cross. An acrostic exercise may be made with "SATISFIED," one letter for each round, "S" touching the earth, and "D" reaching into the clouds, **SALVATION** being the first word, etc. The ladder may also be used with Rom. v, 3–5. Or the word "DEATH" may form an acrostic for the rounds of the ladder: "**D**ying, **E**nriched, **A**ngel's Food, **T**riumphant, **H**eaven." At the base of the ladder write "A little while;" above the ladder write "Evermore." If used for the death of a child, illustrate it by the story of the child raised by Elisha, 2 Kings iv, 18, etc. Write above the exercise "It is well."

One of the following verses may also be used on such an occasion on the board:

> From the group of little faces
>   One is gone;
> In the old, familiar places,
>   Sad and lone,
> Father, mother, meek-eyed brother
>   Sit and moan.

Weep not when ye tell the story
Of the dead;
'TIS A SUNBEAM JOINED THE GLORY
OVERHEAD,
" For of such sweet ones is heaven,"
Jesus said.

_____

" Who plucked that flower? " said the gardener
As he passed through the garden.
His fellow-servant answered " The Master,"
And the gardener held his peace.

_____

The baby wept :
The mother took it from the nurse's arms,
And soothed its griefs and stilled its vain alarms,
And baby slept.

Again it weeps ;
And God doth take it from the mother's arms,
From present pain and future unknown harms—
And baby sleeps.

The Shield of Faith.

This exercise, by J. B. Phipps, of Indianapolis, can readily
be understood by all :

THE PRODIGAL'S

The prodigal comes trembling

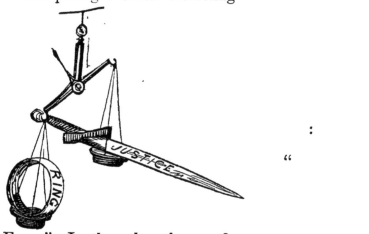

:

"   "

Fame." In the other the words
of a cross. Jesus outweighs all.

LACK OF LOVE.

Or illustrate Rev. ii, 4, by making the outline of the balances, and put in the side that is up,

THY WORKS.
LABOR.
PATIENCE.
RIGHTEOUS HATRED.

In the other balance put the words "God's Requirements—
LOVE." Then print above "Weighed in," and below "Found
wanting of thy first love."

THE BIBLE OUTWEIGHS ALL OTHER BOOKS.

In the outweighed side of the balances put eight or ten
books, with the motto beside them, "Of making books there
is no end." On the other scale put the Bible, with the motto
beside it, "Search the Scriptures."

Things whose worth or desirableness are to be compared,
things between which men hesitate to choose, and things that
are to be tested, may be appropriately represented in the outline balances.

JUDGE

THE GOLDEN RULE.

Simply,	Theref
Implicitly,	All
Honestly,	Things
Tenderly,	Whatso
Slowly,	Ye
Intelligently,	Would
Devotedly,	That
Nobly,	Men
Ably,	
Manfully,	
Mercifully,	To
Openly,	You,
Cautiously,	Do
Sincerely,	
Unbiased,	
Soberly,	
Exactly,	
Justly.	

THE CHRISTIAN'S MONUMENT.

The Christian's monument, as in the Catacombs, may be
inscribed "*Vivit*," for "*He lives*," in a better and truer sense

than ever before. The day of death among the early Christians was marked on the grave-stones "*Natalis dies*," "the
day of birth." A dying girl, just before her death, looked

upward and said softly, " Lift me higher! lift me higher! "
Her parents raised her up with pillows ; but she faintly said,
" No, not that ; but *there !* " again looking earnestly toward
heaven, whither her happy soul fled a few moments later. On
her grave-stone the words are carved, " Lifted higher."

A German infidel had taught his family that man dies as the
beast dies, and has no immortality. His daughter, dearly
loved by her father, died. The custom in Germany is to put
on the grave-stones at the top, " *Hier ruhet in Gott,*" " Here
rests in God ; " but, knowing he had not believed in immortality, those who made the stone came to him and asked what
they should put on. He struggled in his thoughts for a few
moments and then said sadly, " Write *Hier ruhet in Gott.*"
Death had conquered his philosophy. "Him that overcometh
will I make a pillar in the temple of my God."

Our Monument of Victory.

Another exercise with a similar monument : make a picture of Bunker Hill monument.
Near the top picture on its face
a cross, with " Jesus " written
at the center. Around it put
the words, " In this sign con-
quer." Below, in large letters,
" Thanks be unto God that giveth us the victory through our
Lord." Here picture the monogram of Christ, if familiar, otherwise write the words, " Jesus
Christ." Below or beside the
monument make this banner :

WHEN I CRY UNTO

THEE,

then shall mine enemies

TURN BACK ;

THIS I KNOW,

For GOD is WITH ME.

This exercise may be used very appropriately in connection with the altar inscribed " Jehovah Nissi," (*My Banner*,) which Moses raised upon a *hill*, after Amalek had been
put to rout. (Exod. xvii, 8–15.)

SATAN AND THE SAVIOUR.

The following exercise is contributed by Rev. **J. M. Free.**
man, and fully explains itself:

INFANT CLASS BLACKBOARD LESSON : *

Visit of the Wise Men to Bethlehem—Matt. ii, 1–12.

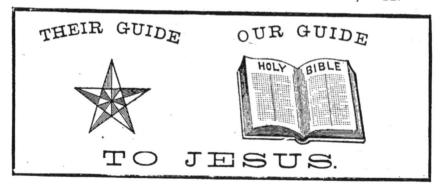

* In using this exercise the teacher can refer to several passages which
speak of the Bible as a guide, as, for instance, Psalm cxix, 105 ; and for the
reverse refer to Prov. xxiii, 26, and parallel passages.

(Reverse.)

THEIR GIFT.	OUR GIFT.
GOLD, Frankincense, Myrrh.	OUR HEARTS.

—*D. B. H.*

TEMPERANCE EXERCISE.

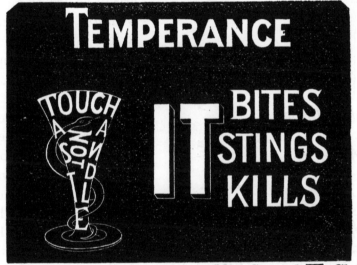

—*Mrs. Samuel W. Clark.*

WATER AND RUM.

Draw a water pitcher, and make on it the following acrostic exercise:

W atchful,
A ctive,
T ruthful,
E xcellent,
R ich.

Then draw some kind of a rum bottle or demijohn, and put **on** it the following :

R uin,
U pas,
M urder,

illustrating the danger of the cup by the story of the Upas tree.—*Rev. J. M. Durell.*

The Steps to Ruin.

A man had committed murder, was tried, found guilty, and condemned to be hung. A few days before his execution,

upon the walls of his prison he drew a gallows, with *five steps* leading up to it.

On the first step he wrote, *Disobedience to Parents.* Solomon says, "The eye that mocketh at his father, and despiseth to obey his mother, the ravens of the valley shall pick it out, and the young eagles shall eat it;" that is, he shall perish by a violent death, he shall come to a miserable, wretched end.

On the second step he wrote, *Sabbath-breaking.* God, in his command, said, "Remember the Sabbath day, to keep it holy." Visit your prisons and jails, and you will find that nine tenths of their inmates have begun their downward course by breaking this command.

On the third step he wrote, *Gambling and Drunkenness.* The late Dr. Nott, having been a close observer of human events, truly says, "The finished gambler has no heart. He would play at his brother's funeral, he would gamble upon his mother's coffin."

Several years ago a youth was hung for killing his little brother. When on the gallows the sheriff said, "If you have any thing to say speak now, for you have only five minutes to live." The boy, bursting into tears, said, "I have to die. I had only one little brother; he had beautiful blue eyes and flaxen hair, and I loved him. But one day I got drunk, for the first time in my life, and, coming home, I found him gathering strawberries in the garden. I became angry with him without a cause, and I killed him at one blow with a rake. I did not know any thing about it till the next morning when I awoke from sleep, and found myself tied and guarded, and was told that when my little brother was found his hair was clotted with his blood and brains, and he was dead. Whisky has done this. It has ruined me. I never was drunk but once. I have only one more word to say, and then I am going to my final Judge. I say it to young people : Never, never, never *touch any thing that can intoxicate !* "

On the fourth step he wrote, *Murder.* God's command is, "Thou shalt not kill."

On the fifth step he wrote, *The Fatal Platform.* It is impossible for us to form a correct idea of the thoughts that must rush through the mind of a man under such circumstances : the disgrace and ignominy attached to his name ; the pains and agony of such a death ; the want of sympathy in the community around him ; the fearful forebodings of his guilty soul at the bar of a holy God.

Thus the way to the gallows is well represented by steps. How emblematic of sin ! Step by step the sinner goes on, until at last the "fatal platform" is reached, and he has to pay the penalty of his misdoing without a single chance of escape.

SAVED THROUGH CHRIST. (Heb. iv, 13–16.)

The following exercise, contributed by Rev. J. S. Ostrander, illustrates at once several of the classes we have mentioned:

The first thought to be impressed is, "All things are naked and open to the eye of Him with whom we have to do." The outline of an eye is made, and opposite is printed the word "Us." The rays from the eye pass to the top and bottom, and also to intermediate points of the word, because God sees us and knows us altogether. Then the words "Judges," "Excludes," "Searches," "Unvails," "Sees," are written one below another between the eye and the word "Us," each of them developed by questions and then explained. But we have "a High Priest, Jesus." Erase the words just written, except their first letters, and the word "Jesus" will remain. Then notice, *God sees us through Jesus.* Write "J" and "T" before and after "Us," and then it will be, GOD SEES US JUST THROUGH JESUS. Illustrate this thought by the following incident:

Little Alice was one of my Sabbath-school scholars—a fair-haired, blue-eyed little girl, whose beautiful face and sweet, winning ways made her a favorite with all. Methinks I can see now the soft, tender look of her mild eyes, fixed so earnestly upon me, as I endeavored to impress upon her opening mind the Gospel plan of salvation.

One day I said to her: "Alice, what will you do when you die, and are called upon to stand before the judgment-seat of God, to answer for all the sins done here upon earth?"

Her face glowed with emotion as she answered, "Christ died for sinners; I will hide behind him. God will not look at me; he will look at Christ."

Beautiful thought, to hide behind Christ, to lose ourselves in him, and, casting aside our own impure works, to rest solely and entirely upon his finished work for salvation!

Illustrations of the thoughts that God *sees, unvails, searches, judges, excludes,* may be found in the following incidents of Scripture: 2 Kings v, 20, etc.; Josh. vii, 1, etc.; Acts v, 1, etc.; Matt. xxvi, 6–25.

CHRIST THE DOOR.—*The Blackboard, (with changes, etc.)*

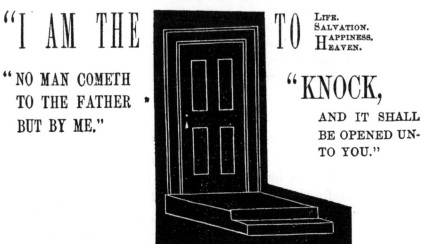

"I AM THE

"NO MAN COMETH
TO THE FATHER
BUT BY ME."

TO

LIFE.
SALVATION.
HAPPINESS.
HEAVEN.

"KNOCK,

AND IT SHALL
BE OPENED UN-
TO YOU."

At the beginning of the exercise "Now" should be written on the door in the center, and "Come unto me" on the steps.

At the close erase " Now," and write " Too late " on the door, and " Depart from me " on the steps.

Another exercise can be made with the door by letting it represent the door to our hearts. In place of the passage " I am the door," etc., write "I stand at the door and knock." At one side write "Be ye lift up, ye everlasting doors; and the King of glory shall come in." On the door write " To-morrow;" on the steps 'write " No admittance except on business." Read the passages on the heart's entrance. Sing " Let the good angels come in," and let some one read or speak the following ·

TO-MORROW.

Lord, what am I, that, with unceasing care,
   Thou didst seek after me—that thou didst wait,
   Wet with unhealthy dews, before my gate,
And pass the gloomy nights of winter there ?
O strange delusion that I did not greet
   Thy blest approach! and O, to Heaven how lost,
   If my ingratitude's unkindly frost
Has chilled the bleeding wounds upon thy feet!
How oft my guardian angel gently cried,
   " Soul, from thy casement look, and thou shalt see
   How He persists to knock and wait for thee! "
And O! how often to that voice of sorrow,
   "To-morrow we will open," I replied,
And when the morrow came I answered still, " To-morrow."
                          —*Longfellow.*

ILLUSTRATION.

" LIE BY TILL MORNING."—Does the reader remember the loss of the vessel called the " Central America?" She was in a bad state, had sprung a leak and was going down, and she therefore hoisted a signal of distress. A ship came close to her, the captain of which asked, through the trumpet, " What is amiss? " " We are in bad repair, and are going down; lie by till morning," was the answer. But the captain on board the rescue-ship said, " Let me take your passengers on board now." " Lie by till morning," was the message which came back. Once again the captain cried, "You had better let me take your passengers on board now." "Lie by till morning," was the reply which sounded through the trumpet. About an hour and a half after the lights were missing, and though no sound was heard, she and all on board had gone down to the fathomless abyss. O unconverted friends, for your souls' sake do not say "Lie by till morning." To-day, even to-day, hear ye the voice of God.

THE RAINBOW OF HEAVEN.

"As in the days of Noah so shall the coming of the Son of man be."

1. The deluge of wrath shall come suddenly. 2 Pet. iii, 10.

2. "Preachers of righteousness" shall warn and invite all to be saved from it. Rev. xxii, 10–12, 17.

3. Christ is our ark; "a hiding place from the wind and a covert from the tempest." Amid the storms of life we are "hid with Christ in God." Jesus gives us the olive branch; "My peace I give unto you," by the "Holy Spirit, heavenly dove." He "shuts us in" from danger. After the "labor"

of life we "enter into rest," as Noah's household rested on
Ararat after long days and nights of tempest; then the
"rainbow round about the throne" shall indicate that "there
remaineth a rest to the people of God." Only those in the
ark "saw the bow in the cloud," and only those who are in
Christ shall see "the rainbow round about the throne." John
iii, 3.

4. As the wicked of Noah's day climbed the mountains to
avoid the angry waters, so at the coming of the Son of man
they shall cry out for "the rocks and hills to hide them from
the wrath of the Lamb." But "none other name is given
under heaven among men whereby we may be saved," except
the ark of Christ.

"COME THOU INTO THE ARK."

5. *The change.* The transient rainbow of earthly hopes
shall be transfigured into the perpetual "rainbow round
about the throne;" the stormy sea of life shall be calmed by
the "Peace, be still" of Christ, into the eternal "sea of glass."
As Noah came from the ark, and built an altar of thanksgiving on the mountain, so God shall show us the meek and lowly
ark of Nazareth, that was "without form or comeliness," re-
built into a golden altar for our perpetual worship.

If you are not "in Christ," you can see in death only the
throne of justice, no rainbow of hope. But the Christian
fears not "the dark waters." A sailor, in the midst of a terrible tempest, was asked why he was not terrified like the
others. "O," said he, "if I sink into the waves I shall only
fall into the hollow of my Father's hand, for he holds all the
waters there." A Christian woman and her child having
been wrecked, were floating about on the spar to which they
were lashed, with little hope of rescue. As a boat at length
came toward them, the sailors, long before they could dis-

tinguish the woman's form, heard these words coming up
through the dashing waves:

> "Jesus, lover of my soul,
> Let me to thy bosom fly,
> While the waters near me roll,
> While the tempest still is high;
> Hide me, O, my Saviour, hide," etc.

These persons were peaceful because they were in the ark.
Like them, let us remember,

> "Other refuge have I none;
> Hangs my helpless soul on Thee," etc.

Ere " the door is shut " *Come thou into the Ark*, and then,
when all the storms of life are past, we can sing as we near
the heavenly mountains of rest:

> "' Land ahead! ' its fruits are waving
> O'er the hills of fadeless green:
> And the living waters laving
> Shores where heavenly forms are seen.

> "Rocks and storms I'll fear no more
> When on that eternal shore.
> Drop the anchor! furl the sail!
> I am safe within the vail!"

CHRIST IN ALL THE SCRIPTURES AND IN ALL TIME.

I. Christ is in all time, before all time, and after all time:
" From everlasting to everlasting " " He was before all
things," " and his throne is for ever and ever." He is " Alpha
and Omega, the beginning and the ending, the first and the
last." The hour-glass representing time, all above it represents the eternity " before his works of old;" all below it that
which shall be when " time shall be no longer."

H. Christ in " all the Scriptures." Luke xxiv, 27. On the
upper border of the hour-glass, which indicates the beginning

of time, begins the Bible record. The heavens and the earth have *only one verse ;* then the earth at large only forty-four verses, and from that point the history narrows itself to the Messianic line. Seth, Noah, *Abraham,* (first covenant,) Judah, *David,* (second covenant,) Mary, and then *JESUS.*

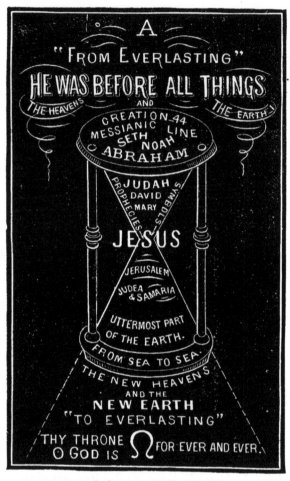

The symbols on the one hand, and the prophecies on the other, also point to Christ. Thus the entire Old Testament narrows from "the heavens and the earth" to the little manger at Bethlehem. But when Christ comes it broadens: "Jerusalem, Judea, and Samaria, the uttermost parts of the earth." Acts i, 8.

At the end of time (lower rim) "his dominion shall be from sea to sea." And when "time shall be no longer," the "new heavens and the new earth," corresponding with "heavens and earth" at the top.

> "Because he never comes, and stands,
> And stretches out to me both hands;
> Because he never leans before
> The gate, when I set wide the door

At morning, or is never found
Just at my side when I turn round,
Half thinking I shall meet his eyes,
From watching the broad moon-globe rise—
For all this shall I cease to pray,
And let my heart grow hard, and say ·
' He perished, and has ceased to be;
Another comes, but never he?'
Nay, by our wondrous being, nay!
Although his face I never see
Through all the infinite To Be,
I know He lives and cares for me."

The symbols and metaphors of the Bible may be outlined on the board, or used as symbol exercises, and the following table may also suggest many exercises to the thoughtful teacher, both for this division, " Outline Exercises," and also for " Symbol Exercises:"

TABLE OF SYMBOLS,

PARTLY OF NEW, PARTLY OF PRIMEVAL SIGNIFICANCE.

The Hieroglyphical Language of the Universal Church during the early ages.

HEAVEN is symbolized by the segment of a circle, sometimes of pure blue, sometimes edged with the thin colors of the rainbow.

THE UNIVERSE by a globe, usually of deep blue.

GOD THE FATHER by a hand issuing from the preceding symbol of Heaven, Ezek. ii, 9; viii, 3.

GOD THE SON by the monogram formed of the initial letters of the name Christ in Greek; also by the Cross, although this was more correctly the symbol of salvation through the atonement; also by a rock, 1 Cor. x, 4; Exod. xvii, 6; also by a lamb, Isa. lvii, 7; frequently with a glory and carrying a cross; also by a pelican, Psa. cii, 6; also by a vine, John xv, 1, etc.; also by a lamp or candle, as " the light of the world," John ix, 5; also by a fish, suggested by the word ἰχθύς, frequently found in the Catacombs, acrostically formed from the initial letters of the titles of Our Saviour, Ἰησοῦς Χριστὸς Θεοῦ υἱὸς Σωτήρ—Jesus Christ, the Son of God, the Saviour.

GOD THE HOLY GHOST by the dove, usually bearing the olive branch; also by water issuing from the beak of the dove, or rising as a fountain from a vase, as the "well of water springing up into everlasting life," John iv, 14; also by a lamp or candlestick, seven of which ranged to the right and left of the altar in the old mosaics, signify the gift of the Spirit. Rev. i, 12; iv, 5.

THE HOLY TRINITY by the three-colored rainbow encircling our Saviour, the visible form or image of the Deity, and who sometimes is represented seated upon it, Ezek. i, 28; Rev. iv, 3; also by three beams of light radiating from the head of Christ; also by the extension of the thumb and fore and middle fingers of our Saviour's hand, as held up in the western form of giving the benediction.

PARADISE by a mountain, in conformity with the traditions of almost all nations.

SATAN by the serpent.

THE OBEDIENCE and ATONEMENT of CHRIST by the cross, sometimes plain, sometimes richly gemmed, occasionally with roses or flowers springing from it.

THE COURSE OF HUMAN LIFE by the sun and moon.

THE CHURCH, in her general character, by a mountain, as typified by Paradise, and in allusion also to Dan. ii, 34.

THE CHURCH MILITANT by a female figure standing, with her hands raised in prayer; also by the vine as "brought out of Egypt," Psa. lxxx, 8; Isa. v, 1, etc.; also by a vessel in full sail—an emblem originally heathen, but naturalized and carried out in the most minute and fanciful particulars by the Latin Fathers.

THE CHURCH TRIUMPHANT by the New Jerusalem, the city of the Apocalypse, Rev. xxi and Ezek. xlvii—frequently identified with the original palace in Eden.

The Two Covenants, the Old and New Testaments, by the " Wheel in the Middle of a Wheel," Ezek. i, 16.

The Sacrament of Baptism, by water poured out on the cross by the dove.

The Lord's Supper, by ears of corn or loaves, and grapes or vases of wine.

The Apostles, by twelve sheep or lambs, usually represented issuing from the cities of our Saviour's birth and death, Bethlehem and Jerusalem, and approaching a central lamb, figurative of Christ, standing on the Mount of Paradise.

The Evangelists, by the four mystic animals described in Rev. iv, 7; Ezek. i, 10, and x, 14, the angel being usually assigned to St. Matthew, the lion to St. Mark, the ox to St. Luke, and the eagle to St. John: also by the four rivers issuing from the Mount of Paradise, " to water the earth," Gen. ii, 10.

The Faithful, by sheep as under the charge of the Good Shepherd, Christ, John x, 14; xxii, 15, etc.; also by fish, as caught in the net of the Gospel, Matt. xiii, 47; Mark i, 17; Ezek. xlvii, 9, and new-born in baptism; also by doves other birds, designs of a loftier and purer element, either eating grapes or ears of corn as figurative of the Eucharist, or drinking from the vase and fountain, emblematical of Christ, or holding branches of olive in their beaks and reposing on the cross: also by stags at the well or water brook, Psa. xlii, 2; also by date trees or cedars, trees of righteousness planted by the waters and bearing fruit in their season, or Psa. i, 3; xcii, 12; Isa. lxi, 3; Jer. xvii, 8; also by little children or *genii* sporting among the vine leaves, or plucking the fruit, and after death, with the wings of Psyche, or the butterfly.

Sanctity, by the *nimbus*, a circlet of glory round the head, a most ancient symbol, being common to the religions of India, Persia, Egypt, Greece, and Rome, from the latter of which it was adopted by the early Christians.

Faith, by the various symbols of the faithful just mentioned.

HOPE, by the anchor, Heb. vi, 19.

CHARITY, by a heart.

PURITY, by the lily.

INCORRUPTIBILITY, by the Rose of Sharon.

WATCHFULNESS, by the cock.

VICTORY, by the palm branch, Rev. vii, 9, or wreath or crown such as was given to the conqueror in the arena, 1 Cor. ix, 25, etc.

PEACE, by a branch or leaf of olive, borne by the dove, symbolical either of the Holy Spirit or of the believer, according to circumstances.

THE RESURRECTION, by the phenix and the peacock, which latter loses its beautiful plumage in winter and recovers it in the spring.

ETERNITY, by a ring or circle of peace, glory, etc., according to the emblematical import of the material of which it is composed, and within which are frequently inserted the symbols of our Saviour, the Church, etc.

ETERNAL LIFE, by the mystic Jordan, the "river which maketh glad the city of God," formed by the junction of the four evangelical streams, descending from the Mount of Paradise, and in which souls, in the shape of little children, are sometimes seen swimming and sporting, precisely as they figure in the mystic Nile, in the tombs of the Pharaohs.

The above table, taken from "Sketches of the History of Christian Art," an excellent work written by Lord Lindsey, is a complete *alphabet of the art language* of the early Church. In almost every case the symbols are derived from the Bible, and form a real alphabet for the eye-teaching that was then so common.

These symbols were grouped in countless combinations, as we combine letters in words. A hand and the symbol of heaven meant "Our Father in heaven." Any of the symbols of Christ with Alpha and Omega on its right and left meant that Christ was "the First and the Last." The fish symbol and the lamb together indicated his divinity and sacrificial character. Faith, hope, and charity, the cross, anchor, and heart, were sometimes mingled. The ring of eternity with the symbol of God or Christ or the Church within, indicates the eternity of that included. In the paintings, sculpture, inscriptions, votive offerings, these symbols were constantly combined into significant forms. In our language to-day these symbols still linger as metaphors.

This table may serve, with a little throwing out of fanciful and useless symbols, and with the symbolism of the tabernacle added, as an *alphabet for the eye-teacher* in object and blackboard teaching. A careful study of the table will suggest many useful exercises to be made by modifications and combinations. To complete the eye-teacher's alphabet we add the symbolism of color, as it has been beautifully brought out in connection with the twelve colors of the heavenly wall, in Rev. xxii, 19, 20.

1. Jasper, (crimson,) passion, suffering.
2. Sapphire, (blue,) truth, calm.
3. Chalcedony, (white,) purity
4. Emerald, (green,) hope.
5. Sardonyx, (mixed color,) tenderness and pain and purifying.
6. Sardius, (blood-red,) love, including anguish.
7. Chrysolite, (golden green,) glory manifest.
8. Beryl, (serenest blue,) bliss.
9. Topaz, (flame,) joy of the Lord
10. Chrysoprase, (azure,) peace that passeth understanding.
11. Jacinth, (purple,) ⎫
12. Amethyst, (purple,) ⎬ promises of future glory.

Of course, only a part of these colors can be used by the blackboard delineator, and he cannot always use them with their appropriate symbolism; but colors have always been types, and some understanding of their import is almost a necessity to any one who would use the blackboard successfully.

The symbolism of color is still more exhibited in Mrs. Jameson's "Legendary Art."

Thus we have spoken of the seven departments of eye-teaching. They should ever be as the seven golden candle-sticks of Revelation, not attracting the eyes of men to themselves, but only revealing the glory of Him who cried from their midst,

"I AM ALPHA AND OMEGA, THE BEGINNING AND THE END-ING, THE FIRST AND THE LAST."

APPENDIX

FOR INFANT CLASS TEACHERS.

BY

MISS SARA J. TIMANUS.

APPENDIX.

EYE-TEACHING IN THE INFANT CLASS.

IT is an acknowledged fact that a child is more the creature of observation than of reflection. Observation may be a simple act of perception, while reflection is the act of continuing thought upon any one subject.

We would not say that a child never reflects, but his habit is rather to observe, than to lay up a store of facts for future reflection: therefore reflection is a more mature development of the mind than observation.

When a child recognizes a fact as the result of a purely mental process we are surprised, and call it precociousness. Little Fred had heard his mamma read that beautiful poem entitled "Katie Lee and Willie Gray," in which occurs the following couplet:

> "Men are only boys grown tall;
> Hearts don't change much after all."

Several weeks after, without question or suggestion from any one, little Fred said, "If men are only boys grown tall, my papa is a boy." The effect of such an assertion was startling coming from the lips of a child five years of age. Why? Because the reflection it involved was unusual. When should we expect a child to begin to reflect? Not as a sudden development, like the unheralded flash of the meteor, but rather as the faint glimmering of light momentarily increasing in intensity and presaging the glorious dawn. Dawning intelligence gathers brilliancy after each exercise of the observing faculties. This is the child's time for reflection. Unlike his elders, his meditations are dependent upon his sur-

13

roundings. · With a child reflection is rarely isolated from observation. A faithful teacher will strengthen this habit. Many ludicrous theories and false dogmas owe their existence to the fact that this point has been too much neglected by educators in the past. In truth, so far has prejudice prevailed that men have met martyrdom for daring to express thoughts which were the results of observation. Memory does not have to go very far back to reach the time when the system of teaching in our public schools almost totally ignored the con-stitution of the child's mind in this regard. Neither is the error wholly obliterated. Under a wrong system pupils are required to commit to memory the rule or text which shall afterward be "explained" or not, as opportunity offers.

Preferable, indeed, is the plan of leading the child through gradual and easy steps, with effort on his own part to acquire the *idea* of the rule or text. After this, if the language he uses to express his thoughts is not choice, that of the book may be substituted. We may doubt that a pupil understands what we endeavor to put into his mind by telling him, but the facts which are evolved from his own consciousness we may know he has fully made his own.

The Sabbath-school teacher adopting this method should *always* finally substitute the exact language of the Book— therein we are forbidden to either take from or add to its words.

God deals with men as with children. In former days they were made daily to observe wondrous exhibitions of his power exercised in their behalf, as the Shekinah, the falling of manna, water being drawn from hard, dry rocks, etc. And to-day God does not ask man to reflect upon his wondrous love without the exercise of observation. Witness each heart, your daily preservation, the beneficent accommodations of nature to your states; but, beyond all, the gift of the be-loved Son, in whom you may observe the attributes of a mer-ciful God and a loving Father.

A person desiring to fit himself to be a teacher of youth, either in the secular school or the Sabbath-school, can have no better course of training than to do faithfully two things: 1. To attach himself lovingly and companionably to a bright child, observing the working of his mind in play. 2. To study God's way of revealing himself to man, since he, indeed, is the highest form of all truth. Such observations may become crystallized into the truisms of a method which shall become a guide in all efforts to instruct. Teachers of Normal classes will have accomplished but little until they have imbued "pupil teachers" with the Spirit of truth-seekers along the two channels named.

Infant-class teacher, are your instructions true to the natural law, that with a child reflection is largely dependent upon observation? If such is the case, you are hardly accustomed to give your little ones "hard pellets of doctrine" in the form of an assignment of verses to learn, until you have rendered them *soluble* by device of illustration which may be dictated by your love and understanding of childhood, guided by a sanctified judgment.*

Accepting the following facts—(1) that a child is the creature of observation; (2) that his habit of observing collects a fund of knowledge upon which he may afterward reflect; (3) that with a child reflection is dependent upon observation—it becomes patent that one who would teach the young should thoroughly understand the observing faculties. Mind comes in contact with matter through the five senses: sight, hearing, touch, smell, and taste. The power of the mind to gain knowledge through these five channels is called the observing faculty. As the mind of the child is most approachable through this faculty, a very important question for the teacher to decide is, through which sense does the mind receive the most complete images? It would

---

* We should advise the person investigating methods to read some works on Mental Philosophy, such as "The Human Intellect," by Professor Porter, or Bain's "Senses and the Intellect."

be impossible to educate wholly through one sense, because objects possess many attributes, all of which cannot be recognized by any one faculty; but this does not preclude the practicability of giving use to one sense above that of the remaining four senses. This question might be tested by considering a group of five persons, each possessing but one of the five senses, and no two of them having the same sense. Which one would have the most intelligent general ideas of things? It seems hardly a debatable question. In touch and taste sensation is limited to actual contact with the object. In smell the object must be near. But that is the case with neither sight nor hearing. How much wider, then, is the plane of their possibilities! To make a still further comparison now between sight and hearing, experience has proven that the eye may take in at a glance mile upon mile of the widely-stretching prairie land, or it may scale the lofty ranges and peaks of distant mountains, existing so far removed in space that the million voices of life which continually make the air resonant are entirely lost to the ear. We claim for sight superior power to any one of the other senses. Let the comparison be continued by considering the attributes of objects discovered by each of the senses.

Smell—Odor.

Taste—Flavor.

Touch—Form, weight, states of being, solid or liquid.

Hearing—Sound, distance, and size, (but imperfectly.)

Sight—Form, color, size, place, distance, weight, (but imperfectly,) states of being, solid or liquid.

If the group of five persons before mentioned should for the first time be brought into contact with a tree, according to the comparison just made between the powers of the five senses, it is evident that the most intelligent idea of the tree would be gained by the person gifted with sight. Teachers have come to recognize the invaluable aid of the eye in their work, and as a result we meet such aphorisms as the following: 1. " The impressions which come to us through

the medium of the eye are ordinarily more distinct and relia-
ble than those which come through hearing." 2. "Truths
associated with familiar objects are made plainer to the mind
and held longer in the memory than when they are taught ab-
stractly." 3. "The unseen must be represented by the seen."

Two of the most popular lecturers of the day, Prof. Agassiz
and Prof. Tyndall, so fully appreciate the advantages of eye-
teaching that they have become noted for their almost
miraculous drawings during lectures. They thus electrify
their audiences to an extent that one not having felt the influence can hardly appreciate. Through the eye they have
been enabled to bring within the grasp of ordinary intelligence facts which are the results of the persevering labor of
gigantic minds. Wishing again to refer to the subject of
drawing as a department of eye-teaching, we will pass over it
for the present.

Although we have given prominence to sight above the
other senses, it would be folly to urge that it should be the
only sense addressed. To do this would bring the teacher's
work down to the level of mere pantomime. We have placed
so much of emphasis on the comprehensiveness of sight more
to prove what a valuable aid eye-teaching may become to
method rather than a method complete in itself. Neither do
we urge that all illustrations shall address the eye. Of course,
"the more senses employed the clearer the perception." It is
not within the province of our present writing to plead for
the exercise of the senses of smell, touch, and taste, but of
sight alone. No one will deny that ordinarily a soul must
hear the message of God to be able to take hold upon salvation, and the only place we ask for eye-teaching is that it may
accompany the _preached word_.

The question next arising is, How may eye-teaching accompany word-teaching? Dear reader, imagine yourself in the
country, and about setting out to walk to the distant home
of a friend. The main highway leading there, in its monotony
and many windings, would become tedious in the extreme; but

if along the side there should be inviting fields, whose grassy surface is covered with mosaics of violets, harebells, anemones, and daisies, forming diagonals in your journey, they would be most grateful to you both in shortening and relieving the tedium of your way. To leave the highway to wander, at the beck of the goddess of pleasure, through those bright fields, would only deter you from the accomplishment of your journey; but when your direct way should lead through them, to follow it would only speed you on. Eye-teaching bears to word-teaching something of the relation of the fields adjacent to the highway. At times the eye becomes a shorter and more direct path toward truth than the ear. To use the method simply to please the child is to abuse it.

Language has been described as " fossil pictures." A person cannot so fully comprehend the beautiful points of a picture by being told what they are as he could do by seeing the picture himself. We would say, then, to the teacher, never use " fossil pictures " when you can have the real pictures. Never attempt to describe an object when the object itself may be procured. We would say to the traveler on the highway, Enter the fields when you can do so to your advantage, otherwise you had better not enter; and to the teacher, Teach through the eye when you can, by thus avoiding the monotony of wordiness, make a direct line from truth to the child's understanding, and not through pleasure of the method lose sight of the grand truths to be inculcated.

It is well understood that eye-teaching accompanied many of our Lord's teachings, and as the Bible is a record of the wonderful lessons he has taught man, it is to the Sabbath-school teacher the very best source from which to gather suggestions for illustration; and, too, the created world is full of hints. God is now daily and hourly teaching man lessons. *

---

* A concordance is invaluable to a person searching the Bible for illustrations. No Sunday-school teacher should be without an unabridged copy.

So much has been written upon this point in preceding chapters it becomes unnecessary to reconsider it here.

To answer fully the question, How may eye-teaching accompany word-teaching? we come naturally to the consideration of two divisions of eye-teaching adapted to the infant class, namely: 1. Object Illustrations; and, 2. Black-board Illustrations.

OBJECT ILLUSTRATIONS.

There is a distinction to be made between the object lesson of the secular school and that of the Sabbath-school. In the first instance it is the aim to stimulate the observing faculties, and to increase general intelligence. In such lessons the following points are usually considered: Names and positions of parts; qualities, uses dependent upon qualities, etc. If the teacher should fortunately be a Christian, some of God's truth will be worked into the lesson; yet it will be secondary to the facts concerning the object. This is as it should be in the secular schools, but to adopt the same method in the Sabbath-school would be to do a great wrong, and every thing which does not promulgate it has no right there. An object may indeed be the subject of a Sabbath-school lesson, not for the purpose of imparting knowledge of the object itself, but that it may become the center around which religious truth shall cluster. The differences which should be made cannot better be illustrated than by presenting two sketches of lessons on the same topic, the first designed for the secular school, the second for the Sabbath-school.

ROCKS.

Parts.	Surface, edges, corners, inner part.
Qualities.	Hard, cold, lasting, color, heavy, dry, sometimes bright, etc.
Uses.	Building houses, foundations of houses, walls, cellars, wells, side-walks, streets bridges, etc.

Uses dependent upon qualities.	For houses, because hard, dry, lasting, heavy, and bright. For cellars, foundations, and walls, because hard, dry, and lasting. For side-walks, bridges, and streets, because hard, dry, heavy, and lasting.
Where found by man.	Under the ground. The different processes of getting rocks out of the ground should be mentioned, and the term quarry given.
Different kinds of rocks shown and named.	If possible, some specimens of the rough material, and carvings of the same, should be shown.
God the maker.	Attention should be directed to the beautiful forms in which rocks appear, as mountains, shelving for cascades, etc., and God spoken of with adoration as their maker.

The foregoing sketch would furnish material for several lessons suitable to children of five and six years of age. This is also the case with the following sketch, designed for the infant class of the Sabbath-school. Neither exercise should be conducted in the form of lectures, but catechetically

ROCKS.

1. *Rocks are hard and dry.* Let the children handle some pieces of rocks, and by the teacher be led to discover and state these two qualities.

Then the story of God causing the hard and dry rock to become a fountain of waters, from which thousands of people quenched their thirst. And an application should be made of the story by teaching that Christ Jesus has become the rock of our salvation. From him we may have eternal life, which is living water. Psa. xcv, 1.

2. *Rocks are lasting.* Develop this fact with the children, by referring them to rocks they have seen which never seem to change, or by comparing rocks with water which either runs away or dries up, or with the grass and flowers which

fade and die. Rocks do crumble although they do not seem to do so. God is more lasting than the rocks. He will be the same forever, therefore he is called The Rock. Psa. lxii, 7.

3. *Certain kinds of birds make their homes in the rocks.* Let the teacher illustrate this by showing a picture, and engaging in an easy and pleasant conversation with the children.

We should think so much about Christ our Rock that we may be said to live with him. Psa. xxxi, 3.

4. *Churches are made of rocks.* God has called his friends "lively stones," with which he will build a holy temple, Christ Jesus being the foundation stone; that is, God will gather together those who love him in his heavenly home for the sake of his dear Son who died to redeem us. Eph. ii, 19–21.

With the aid of a concordance many additions might profitably be made to this sketch.

Let us compare the probable thoughts of two children walking among rocks after having received the two series of lessons just given.

The child from the secular school would try to find rocks like those which had been shown him at school; according to the different degrees of hardness, he would decide which would make the best houses, streets, walks, etc.; he would examine the marks on the rocks to discover how they had been gotten out of the quarry. When his feet should be hurt or his shoes cut by coming in contact with the rocks, he would think of edges and corners. It is more than probable that such thoughts as these would occupy him to the exclusion of godly meditation.

The mind of the other child, under the same circumstances, instead of dwelling upon the things of earth, would be carried upon the ladders of simile up to his God. Just this result is the aim of the object lesson in the Sunday-school. A strong point has been gained when religious truth becomes thus associated with every day experiences. Then, indeed, shall we dwell in the crevices of the Rock.

There is yet another distinction to be made—now between the object lesson and the object illustration. An exercise may contain several object illustrations and still not be an object lesson. The subject of the object lesson is an object, and the aim is to so associate truth with it that at the very mention of its name the soul will unfold itself toward God.

When object illustrations are used, the subject may be either biographical, topical, or historical; the objects being used to develop the thoughts of the lesson with vividness. The infant class teacher should take advantage of such illustrations in nearly every lesson. It would be well, if practicable, to exhibit each object mentioned in the lesson. Little folks, from the fact that ordinarily so little religious instruction is given in homes, are apt to fail in some measure to recognize objects named by the teacher as those which they are accustomed to see. Considering the novelty of the time. place, and instruction, this should not excite wonder. How can the error better be corrected than by bringing the objects themselves where they may be seen. Truly the end sought dignifies the effort.*

The aim of both the object lesson and the object illustration is to impress the truth; the former by association, the latter by assistance toward development of the lesson.

As truth is to be associated with the object in the object lesson, the object itself should remain before the class during the entire lesson time, and the eyes of the children should oftentimes be directed toward it, but with the object illustration it should be different. When the thought has been developed by its aid the object should be quietly laid away, its work has been accomplished, and to leave it longer in view would only detract from the impression the lesson should make upon the mind and heart. Intended only to throw light upon

---

* The lessons following this article will be found to embody our idea of object illustrations. Also in preceding pages suggestions on this point may be found in "Stories Represented."

the understanding, if still retained in sight, its effect in oblit-
erating the lesson would be somewhat like the effect of the
sun's rays resting too long on the sensitive plate in the camera,
which, in their power, will cover all with blackness and destroy
the image.

The teacher is in danger of committing several errors in
the use of object illustrations, one of which has just been
noted, that of retaining the object in sight when there is no
further use for it, thus inviting the attention to wander.

Another error is to fail in making a distinction between the
illustration and the truth. The laughable story has been told
of a child who had been taught to sing in the Sunday-school
a song containing this sentiment, " Let me die with the harness on." We will not stop to criticise the appropriateness
of the expression. Evidently the child had not been taught
that by "harness on" was meant, in the exercise of sweet
Christian graces, which, in language adapted to the child,
would be, living a godly life, working for the Lord. In other
words, the child had not been taught the spirit of the song,
as he was heard to sing " Let me die in the harness shop."
We called it a *laughable* story ; we beg leave to change the
adjective and call it a lamentable story. Far better would it
be never to attempt illustration than to create such mental
confusion. We should fear that by such teaching the child
might lose his way to heaven's shore. It is like throwing dust
into eager young eyes that are seeking the Way of Life. Make
an illustration practical or make none at all. Probe the minds
with questions to test whether or not the children are able to
make practical application of the truth which the illustration
teaches. This should always be the last step in the use of an
illustration. For instance, the evidences of a nearness to
Christ might thus be taught. Require the children to touch
some pieces of heated iron, (simply warm.) How are the
pieces of iron? Warm. Because they are warm, where do
you know they have been? Near the fire. Why does fire
make iron warm? Because there is heat in the fire.

When Jesus was on the earth he was always loving every one. Of what feeling do you think his heart was full to make him so? Love. Say after me, Fire is full of heat. Jesus' heart is full of love. When is iron full of heat? When it has been near the fire. Trying to be just like Jesus we call living near to him. Of what feeling is Jesus' heart full? Love. What feeling will people who try to live near Jesus have in their hearts? Love. Say after me, When iron has been near the fire it is full of heat. When people live near Jesus their hearts are full of love. (Lay the iron aside.) The love in Jesus' heart made him do some good for every body. How may you know when people are trying to live near Jesus? When they try to do good for every body. Where does the iron get heat? From the fire. Where may we get love enough to do good for every body? From Jesus. What do we call living near to Jesus? Trying to be like him. You may name some one who, you think, is trying to live near Jesus.

Without the emphasis given the truth in the preceding lesson by appealing to experience, doubtless children would in some indefinite way conclude that the love of Christ is a fire, imparting heat, or that perhaps our bodily warmth is imparted by dwelling in nearness to Jesus.

Let a teacher never be satisfied in using an illustration without investigating thoroughly the impression made by it on the minds of the children. For this reason, as well as many others, the practice of giving the lesson beforehand to a class of children comparing with those for whom the lesson is designed, is invaluable.

Still another error in the use of an object illustration is to treat of it too exhaustively. It should be the aim to teach but one truth in each lesson, and only such attributes as are relevant to that truth should be considered. In the lesson just given upon the evidences of living near to Christ, much might have been said about the piece of iron; but the only quality which had a bearing upon the truth of the lesson was *heat.* Consequently, heat was the only quality which was permitted to claim the attention of the children. The object illustration is valuable only so far as it aids in developing a thought; beyond this, to talk of it becomes detrimental, for two reasons principally: 1. It exhausts the time, leaving little or no opportunity for the real purpose of the hour. 2. It divides the mental forces. By introducing thoughts foreign to the lesson, although they may be properly suggested by the object, the teacher's efforts are rendered futile. In mental as well as in physical states, power can only be secured by concentration.

The object lesson is in one sense figurative, but its right use should partake more of the nature of the simile than of the metaphor. In the simile comparison is expressed, but in the metaphor it must be inferred. It requires a degree of intellectual culture to understand a metaphor. An untutored, undeveloped mind will accept the metaphorical statement in a literal sense. Credulity, that lovely characteristic of childhood, only increases the dangers of metaphorical teaching. The child, from his very nature, will accept the exact words of his teacher as indisputable truth, therefore the teacher should be careful to let the unadorned truth make the last impression upon the mind. Infant class teachers are in danger of connecting with the object illustration such sublime thoughts that it will not be possible to translate them in a sufficiently literal sense to be comprehended by children. The teacher must not presume that which is clear to his understanding may also be made so to a child. Beyond the usual advantage which an adult mind possesses, as a Christian there is an increased advantage, which is a God-given insight into the spiritual sense of things; and it must not be expected that little children, with their comparatively weak intellects, and without God's converting grace in their hearts, will be able to understand the highest conceptions of a mature and divinely intensified mind.

Apropos to this point are some remarks once made in a

convention of Sunday-school workers which are in substance as follows: If a child should be perfectly familiar with the form and appearance of a dog, but entirely unacquainted with a horse, never having seen a horse nor a picture of it, what would be the result of some one trying to give him an idea of a horse by simply describing it? If the child should be so gifted with the power to draw that he could place upon paper the conception of his mind, what would be the form of his ideal horse? An animal very much resembling the dog, but very little like the horse. In the language of the speaker, "a dog with a long head."

It is an immutable law that ideas gained through conception must be based upon similarities. It might be urged that to describe differences would give a true mental picture. Conception based upon dissimilarities can at best give one but negative ideas. Correct images are formed in the mind either through the aggregate of resemblances or by observation, therefore the teaching in arranging illustrations should apply these two test questions: Is my illustration related to the common experience of childhood? or shall I be able by this means to bring this truth within the range of the observing faculties? If neither plan is practicable, it will be safe to conclude that the illustration is beyond the comprehension of the childish intellect and is therefore not fit to be used. The teacher should continually imagine himself in the place of the child, not measuring himself to get an estimate of the child's powers.

Not alone should the teacher endeavor faithfully to adjust the illustration to the child's understanding, but the point of whether or not the child has enjoyed the bit of experience which is proposed to be used is hardly second in importance to the matter of understanding. Just as a piece of white cloth immersed in unclean water will become soiled, so will a truth be impressed with the moods or states of a mind at the time of its reception. Thus the law of similarities should be applied to the affections or moral states as well.

Finally, to briefly sum up the ideas advanced upon the subject of object illustration. The aim of the object lesson of the secular school is to stimulate the observing faculties and increase general intelligence; whereas in the Sunday-school the design is to accustom the mind to habits of religious thought through the observing faculties. Object lessons and object illustrations should not be confused. In the object lesson the end sought is to make of the object a kind of spiritual magnet around which holy truths shall cluster. The object illustration is for the purpose of so increasing the light upon a certain point of truth that it can be more readily comprehended. Its use should be but momentary. The fewer illustrations used to illuminate our point the better. Many different illustrations do not increase simplicity, but rather produce complexity of ideas. In the object lesson, since the aim is to associate truth, the object should be kept before the class during the entire lesson. The object illustration, its use being merely to develop a thought, should be laid away when its part is done.

The following errors are most readily committed in the way of object illustrations: 1. To retain the object in sight when its work has been accomplished. 2. To neglect to aid the class in making a practical discrimination between the illustration and the truth. 3. To endeavor to make an object lesson out of every object illustration. 4. To make the illustration so sublime by its appeal to the spiritual apprehension that a child cannot grasp its significance.

BLACKBOARD ILLUSTRATIONS.

An idea will not be checked, but struggles for expression. If a thought seems valuable to us, we not only desire to express it, but we wish to give it force, that our hearers may be impressed with the same degree of intensity that we ourselves feel. The earnest Sabbath-school teacher has both the thought to communicate and the desire to do it with force. A teacher of adult classes finds ready resource in the use of an extended vocabulary, but the infant class teacher must necessarily be limited to the use of few words, because young children have meager attainments in language. Illustrations with objects and with the blackboard may happily supply this deficiency. Not that children shall thus be relieved from expressing their thoughts, but that by illustration ideas may be conveyed to them that through their feeble powers of language they could not grasp. Thus a demand for new terms is created. These should be given by the teacher. Pupils in this way are led to use language intelligently which at first they could not comprehend.

The blackboard, too, gratifies the child's love of pictures, and they like fresh pictures too. Novelty is to them full of charms. To meet this desire for variety with appropriate cuts and engravings would prove more expensive than practicable. We do not wish to seem to underestimate the value of large cuts or pictures. Just here there has been a want long unsupplied; until recently the only kind of pictures at all appropriate has been a series of English Scripture charts, and these were too expensive for general use. To be available a cut should be large enough and sufficiently distinct to be used hanging up, or in the hand of the teacher, not having to be passed among the children to be seen. A series of sketches illustrating the Scriptures, large, distinct, and inexpensive, though not rude or common, would be a valuable aid for some artist to give to the Sunday-school cause.

However, no infant class should be without a blackboard. At first glance the matter of representation seems a formidable part for the teacher to perform. If we take advantage of the strong imaginative powers of children, we shall soon discover that it will answer nearly as well to represent people and journeys, or places, by dots and lines as by elaborate drawings. In proof of this, let the teacher remember that a child at play invests an old and broken toy with all the attributes of something new and beautiful, and seemingly gets just as much enjoyment from it as if it were new and beautiful.

Chairs are converted into a railroad train. A journey on a hobby-horse is full of delights, although the horse continually goes but never proceeds! Taking advantage of this peculiarity of childhood, the teacher has comparatively an easy task to use the blackboard.

In preceding chapters many suggestions have been made in regard to materials, the use of the blackboard, etc., which will be found just as helpful to infant class teachers as to those of any other grade. It becomes, therefore, quite unnecessary at this juncture to offer hints upon the same points.

The blackboard work of the infant class may be divided into two classes, Pictorial Illustration and Lettering. We will now consider each of these divisions separately.

PICTORIAL ILLUSTRATION.

It has been urged that only outlines are needed in drawing pictures upon the blackboard in connection with the Sunday-school teacher's work, that fineness of detail is not desirable, as it renders the picture less distinct when viewed from a distance.

A Sunday-school teacher seeing the force of this argument, but feeling powerless to execute the telling outlines, made application to an artist for a course of lessons in outline drawing. The marvelous use Professor Agassiz makes of a few lines was cited as something like the power and facility desired to be obtained. But, alas! it proved that the apparent simplicity was the touch of a master hand! The reply was, The power of giving to one line the expression of many lines is the very highest art. Its apparent simplicity is deceiving. The beginning of such an acquirement is to be made in representing a very simple object: for instance, a string curved in different ways might be represented, first by looking at it, then from memory. After this an object with very simple outlines, such as a leaf, should be drawn in the same way, first from sight, then from memory. Gradually the subject of the

14

sketch should become more and more complicated. After a short time a return should be made to simple objects to be outlined entirely from memory. It was also said that tact and rapid execution in outlining could not be gained by the mere copyist. Ruskin says the true way to learn to draw is not by copying pictures, but by representing objects.

Why should not the Sabbath-school teacher be as desirous to draw well as he is to question well? We are satisfied that in neglecting to do it great power is sacrificed. It is true, we have recommended the use of lines and dots, (those who cannot draw will find great satisfaction in this method;) but it is undeniably true that outline pictures would be more enjoyed by the children, and for this reason produce a better effect than lines and dots. If the teacher attempts drawing at all, it should be well done. It is altogether wrong to violate the æsthetic tastes of children, and to associate God's perfect truth with that which is misshapen and deformed. If a teacher has not mastered the art of drawing, by beginning early in the week, through patient practice, he should be able to make one illustration in an acceptable manner. It is our opinion that Sunday-school teachers have hardly been sufficiently careful about the quality of their representations. It is a matter that demands earnest attention.

The plan of having the drawings made beforehand has been advocated by many. The interest of the children in a picture made in their presence would be far greater than in one previously drawn. In one case the impression would be passive, in the other active. The rapid use of the crayon enlists the interest of the children, and has great influence in fixing their attention. If the teacher's effort at the blackboard is slow and engrossing, the magnetism of the controlling mind is lost. This thought is applicable as well to lettering.

LETTERING.

In the primary department of a secular school, a teacher, wishing to break up the dull monotony of the reading lesson, conceived the idea of printing upon the blackboard original compositions of words contained in the reading book. The teacher was entirely unaccustomed to blackboard lettering. Distinctness and rapidity of execution were the two attainments which she sought for herself, and the skill gained in a short time was surprising. The sentences on the blackboard were read by the little ones with a delight and animation quite in contrast with their former plodding manner.

The teachers of the Sunday-school infant class may make an application of this incident by resolving to learn to print rapidly, in order to put upon the blackboard short sentences expressive of any step or point in the lesson, or the name of persons or places mentioned, and the Golden Text. To require the entire work on the blackboard to be read at the close of the lesson would form a good summary, thus leaving the truth of the lesson arranged in logical and concise statements. Through such a method the understanding would be helped, and the memory greatly aided. It is not likely that the majority of children in infant classes will be able to read rapidly from the blackboard; a few will, however. These few, and the teacher, can guide the others along, who will probably read the idea of the word rather than the words themselves. The printed rather than the script form of the letters has been advised, for the reason that more children will be able to read the former than the latter.

A small blackboard at home would afford the teacher many hours of pleasant and profitable employment. A few minutes devoted to practice each day would enable one to use the crayon with decided advantage in the Sunday-school.

There is an attractive as well as unattractive way of doing almost every thing. It is so with lettering. A little variation in color and form will be attractive to the child, because it will gratify his love of variety and change. In preceding pages many suggestions to aid in introducing the desired variety will be found in Initial, Motto, and other kinds of lessons, which will be helpful to infant class teachers. In the few lessons immediately following this article directions will also be found for the use of the blackboard.

We wish to present still another phase of eye-teaching, not in relation to object or blackboard illustrations, but the influence of the teacher's eye upon the pupils. Has the reader ever experienced the unpleasant sensation of listening to a speaker whose glance was habitually raised above the level of the audience? or, perhaps, been a listener when the gaze of the speaker was rambling, not being fastened anywhere for a moment. In either case the effect was disagreeable. There is so much egotism in humanity that each individual must in some way feel himself recognized to receive definite impressions. A pre-eminently successful speaker once gave his experience in this regard, and it was to the effect that he always selected two or three persons in various places in his audience to whom to preach his sermon. He said, "In this way I make each one of my hearers feel that I have something to say to him." There is a power in this thought which the Sabbath-school teacher should reduce to practice. The infant class teacher, particularly, should endeavor to make each little one feel the influence of his eye.

In closing we cannot but express the wish that these few hints to infant class teachers may lead many to adopt eye-teaching in their work. And may the few thoughts which have been offered strengthen and encourage those who have already found eye-teaching to be an invaluable aid.

We wish you all God-speed in your labors with the little ones of the fold.

The Widow's Oil Increased. 2 Kings iv, 1–15.

Golden Text. Matt. v, 6.

Point. Only through grace given us by God can we live righteously.

SYNTHETIC STEPS DEVELOPING THE POINT.

1. By Elisha's help the widow satisfied her creditor.

2. Through the gift of the Spirit we are enabled to please God.

METHOD IN DETAIL.

First Step. What name do we give to a woman whose husband has died? The Bible tells us of a widow who owed some money to a man. She was poor. Could she pay the debt? Because she had no money to give the man he said, " I will take your two sons and they shall be my slaves." That poor widow went to Elisha, a man whom God had made very wise, and she told him all her trouble. I will read to you from the Bible what Elisha and the widow said to each other. (2 Kings iv, 2.) What one thing had she that she might sell and get money? Could she have gotten enough money in that way to pay her debt? No, ma'am. God helped Elisha to make a way for the widow to pay her debt! You may all think a moment how it was done, but I shall not ask you to tell me. Now I will tell you. Elisha told the widow to go to her neighbors and borrow many empty cups and jugs, to set them in her house, to take her little pot of oil, and to pour the oil from it into the many jars. (Let the teacher take in her hand a small vessel of water and place several empty jars in sight, saying, We will try to do as the poor widow did, that is, to fill these many empty jars with what is in the little cup; but I will use water instead of oil. Teacher pours the contents of the cup into one jar which is not then filled. Children led to observe this. How could doing so help the poor widow? (Children speculate.) Would it not be very strange if, as fast as I should pour water out of this cup more should come in, itself, until there would be enough to fill all of these empty jars?

The widow did as Elisha had told her, and began to pour the oil from the little pot, and the oil kept coming and coming until the jars were full! How would this oil help the widow to pay her debt? She could sell it. Who of you would like to hear me read the story of the widow from the Bible? (This is desirable if there is time. Put the objects out of sight.)

Second Step. What does God do for you? "He gives us breath all the time, fruit to eat, bright flowers to see. He makes things grow so that we may have things to eat and clothes to wear." I think of something greater than these. He has given his dear Son to die for us, so that we can go to heaven. We all owe God a great debt of love. God does not ask us to pay him, but what kind of acts does he want us to give him? Loving right acts. Listen, each child, if what I tell you is true. Some time you have promised yourself and mamma that all through the day you would not do a naughty act. For an hour or so you did very nicely, then you seemed to lose your good spirit and did wrong. All who think this is true may raise their hands. I think you are somewhat like the widow. She did not have oil enough of her own to fill the jugs, and you have not enough good spirit to fill all the days with loving right acts for God. Let the teacher now draw on the blackboard seven little jugs and say, Here is a little jug for each day in the week; let us place the letters for each day under them. (See chart.) Now I will

draw a picture of the heart from which we are to fill each day, (pointing to jugs,) full of loving right acts for God. (See chart.) Could the widow fill all of the empty jugs with only the oil she had put into her little pot? Neither can we, dear ones, fill all our days with the little good spirit *we* may put into our hearts. But if we pray to God he will give us more and more of the Holy Spirit until we shall be able to fill all our days with loving right acts. I will read you what God has promised about this. (Teacher, read Matt. v, 6, from the Bible; print same on blackboard. Children, read it in concert.)

BLESSED ARE THEY WHICH DO HUNGER AND THIRST AFTER RIGHTEOUSNESS, FOR THEY SHALL BE FILLED.

THE WATERS HEALED. 2 Kings ii, 19–25.

Golden Text : John iii, 16.

Point. To teach that although Jesus came to give life to all, he may be made the "savor of death unto death."

SYNTHETIC STEPS DEVELOPING THE POINT.

1. According to our own acts a blessing will yield either joy or pain.

2. Elisha was the cause of life to some but death to others.

3. Unbelief in Jesus, who came to give life, will yield death.

METHOD IN DETAIL.

First Step. (Let the teacher show some object intended to bring comfort or pleasure which through abuse was made to yield pain : For instance) : Here is a little saw ; it belongs to a set of tools which I gave to a dear little boy, thinking he would be made very happy, but in a short time he had cut his finger with the saw, which caused him pain. Did the saw make the boy sad or glad ? Was it the fault of the saw that it did not make him happy ? What was the trouble ? He did not use the saw right. Can you remember something given to you to bring you pleasure which only gave you trouble, because you did not use it right ? (Permit a few replies. Print on the blackboard the first two sentences of the chart, and ask the children to read them.)

Second Step. You learned last Sunday about two men. Who can tell their names ? Which was the wiser ? How much wiser ? In the country where Elisha lived the water in the streams had nearly dried up, and what was left became very bad, so that the plants would not grow. As nothing would grow, what would happen to the people ? Some of the men in that country knew that Elisha had been made wise like Elijah, so they thought they would ask him to heal the water. Elisha told them to bring a new jug with salt in it; then he went to where the waters began and threw in the salt, asking God to help him heal the waters, and so God did. After that the plants grew, and the land was beautiful and green. Would the people die now? Who was the cause of giving them life? Elisha. Why? Because he healed the waters.

Just after Elisha had healed the waters he was passing along the road, when many persons came out and said very ugly words to him. He asked God to punish them, and out of the woods near by God sent two bears. What do you think the bears would do? Kill them. Yes, they tore in pieces forty-two of those bad people. Who was the cause of their death? Elisha. Had he given death when he had healed the waters? No, life. All say after me, Elisha gave life to some, but death to others. Whose fault was it that he gave death to some? It was the fault of the wicked people themselves. When I think of Elisha giving both life and death, I think, too, of this little saw which will either give joy or pain according to the way it is used. To whom does the saw give pain? To whom did Elisha give death?

Third Step. God sent his own dear Son into this world to die, that by his dying we might have a home in heaven. Some people do not care about this; others say, " Jesus is our best friend." God has said those who do not love Jesus shall have sorrow and pain forever. To whom does Jesus give joy? What two things will this little saw give? (showing it.) Will it give joy or pain to you? Joy, if we use it right; pain, if we use it wrong. What two things did Elisha give? Life and death. Whose fault was it that he gave death?

Little ones, Jesus came into this world to give us all heav-enly joy; but because some people will not believe what he promises he gives them everlasting sorrow and pain. If you would get sweet joy from Jesus instead of pain, what must you do? Remember, each little child, that it rests with you whether Jesus will be life or death to you. (Teacher, read Golden Text from the Bible, print it upon the blackboard, and require the children to read it together.)

CHART.

Right use brings joy,
Wrong use brings pain.

FOR GOD SO LOVED THE WORLD THAT HE GAVE HIS ONLY BE-GOTTEN SON, THAT WHOSOEVER BELIEVETH IN HIM SHOULD NOT PERISH, BUT HAVE EVERLASTING LIFE.

ACCOUNTABILITY TO GOD. Rom. xiv, 7–13.

Golden Text. Rom. xiv, 12.

Point. The judgment which each and all must receive.

SYNTHETIC STEPS DEVELOPING THE POINT.

1. A copy to imitate and judgment passed. 2. Living after Christ our copy, (a partial review.) 3. God's judgment upon the life lived.

CHART.

Loving.	Lowly.	Meek.
Selfish.	Proud.	Revengeful.

METHOD IN DETAIL.

First Step. Let the teacher show a page of some old copy-book, saying that a little boy or girl wrote it. The marks are so small that you cannot see them, so I will try to make some just like them on the blackboard. I will first write as the teacher did on the line at the top of the page, which we call the copy. (See chart.) The little boy's task was to make marks just like those his teacher had made. He made some like this one (first on chart.) Do you think he was sitting still or moving about when he made marks like this?

I see many marks like this one (second on chart.) Was the boy trying hard, or did he not care when he made such a mark as this one? He did not care. This mark (third on chart) looks much like those the teacher has made. I will tell you why. Sometimes his teacher would come up behind him, and take hold of his fingers and gently guide them. When the little boy had written his page full, to whom do you think he would have to show it? To his teacher. I have been in a room where many children were writing in their copy-books, and when a large bell would be rung we all had to put our pens down and wait for the teacher to look at our writings. Each mark on this page (pointing to it) has told its story to the teacher. How? By its looks. When did the little boy show his page to the teacher?

Second Step. We learned several Sabbaths ago just how good God wants us to be. Teacher and children recite together the Golden Text of July 21. In what way does God show us how perfectly good he is? By sending his dear Son into this world. If, then, we would try to be somewhat like God, whom must we have for our copy? Jesus. The more we do as Jesus did, the more we shall be like God. What was Jesus' heart full of to every body? Love. Then he was loving. (Teacher, print *loving*.) Was he loving to the poor and the beggars? What shall we say of him because he was? (Print lowly.) Did he strike or harm any one who hurt him? How was he, then? Meek. (Print *meek*.) Let us now read the copy by which we must live. Instead of being loving to every one, we are selfish; we are not lowly but proud; we are not meek, because we want to hurt those who hurt us; we are not meek but revengeful. (See chart; let the teacher print while talking.) Did the little boy write much like the copy? (pointing to blackboard.) Do we live like our copy? When did the boy make the best marks? When the teacher guided his hand. And so we shall live nearer as God wants us to live, if we pray for the help of the Holy Spirit.

Third Step. When was the boy called on to show his page to the teacher? When we have lived all our days God will call us before him to tell him of our lives. Just as plainly as we see the marks on this page, so shall all the acts we have ever done be where God can see them. We said that each mark here tells its story about the boy, so will each act we have done tell its story about us to God. Every one must come thus before God. Here is a verse in the Bible that tells us so. (Teacher read the Golden Text; afterward print it on the blackboard; children read,) "Every one of us shall give an account of himself to God." Rom. xiv, 12.*

---

* The three preceding lessons have been published in the "National Sunday-School Teacher," in the regular course of infant class lessons arranged for that periodical by Miss Timanus.

BIBLICAL INDEX.

ALPHABETICAL INDEX.

Lightning Source UK Ltd.
Milton Keynes UK
UKHW02f0416080518
322246UK00013B/802/P

9 781331 806776